LIFTING OUR VOICES

LIFTING OUR VOICES

Readings in the Living Tradition

Unitarian Universalist Association

Boston

Printed in the United States

Cover design by Suzanne Morgan
Text design by Jeff Miller

Special thanks to Julie Parker Amery for her help with the thematic song pairings, organization, and index.

ISBN: 978-1-55896-749-6

6 5 4 3 2 1
18 17 16 15

Library of Congress Cataloging-in-Publication Data

Lifting our voices : readings in the living tradition.
   pages cm
  Includes index.
  ISBN 978-1-55896-749-6 (pbk. : alk. paper) 1. Unitarian Universalist Association—Liturgy—Texts. 2. Public worship. 3. Worship programs. I. Unitarian Universalist Association.
  BX9853.L54 2014
  264'.09132—dc23
                              2014033714

Contents

Preface

"Love one another and always tell the truth."

So advised Jan Hus, the fifteenth-century religious reformer and martyr. The power of these and other ancient words remains vivid today, while at the same time, each generation discovers new ways of speaking more deeply its understanding of love and truth.

Like our ancestors, we seek in times of worship together, as well as in private contemplation, to lift up these great goals to illuminate the challenges that confront our days. We who would move boldly through a world of consumerism, belligerence, entitlement, suffering, and far too often, bloodshed, seek words that will allow us to offer witness, consolation, encouragement, and transcendence to ourselves and others.

The biblical psalms used by our ancestors in their lengthy worship services provided them with memorable, literate phrases. By giving voice to the shared reality of the inner life, these elegant words could often redeem the week before or prepare the people to embody them in the week ahead. Many of these lines still echo in our language: "deep calling unto deep," "commune with your own heart . . . and be still," "the sorrows of death encompassed me," "of whom shall I be afraid?" "truth shall spring out of the earth," "blest is the one who considers the poor," and "joy cometh in the morning."

But as the generations rise and fall, the wars of the past are surpassed by the wars of the present age. Prosperity and poverty diverge in new ways, and new technology remakes the world in ways Waldo Emerson, Kenneth Patton, Olympia Brown, or Francis Watkins Harper could hardly have comprehended. New words of love and truth, new memorable phrases, new encouragements are in order. Assumptions, sometimes unconsciously made in previous eras, have been challenged and rethought.

Contemporary voices in this new century still revere both love and truth and find ways in worship of moving out of the familiar and into new territory. Styles of imagery and poetry that might have startled our ancestors encourage us to live out lives of depth.

Because each of our congregations, each of our ministers, lay leaders, and chaplains, is free to craft the art of worship in relationship to, but often transcending, received traditions, the readings in this supplement may be used in a variety of ways.

We hope you will suggest to each other ways to take the beautiful but still raw materials of this book and craft them into celebrations of life and love that will deepen the lives of members of our congregations, our friends and visitors, and our colleagues, or any to whom we minister, such as patients, prisoners, and military personnel.

Our literate and living tradition may look a lot different from this book by the time the next generation dawns. Perhaps such memorable and redeeming words will be offered in ways we cannot now imagine; perhaps the unconscious assumptions made by our generation will by then seem obvious to later religious progressives.

But this is our era, our time, and we offer you these rich and varied resources as timely ways to remind us all of our enduring task, to "love one another and always tell the truth."

WORSHIP READINGS COMMITTEE
Mark Belletini
Kendyl Gibbons
Angela Herrera
Abhi Janamanchi
Hope Johnson

Worship Tips

We are a unique and diverse people. A living community of shared ways, and yet with distinct worship practices, none of which is universal.

In our living tradition, each congregation, each open circle of celebration, *shares* a few common practices with all the others. These are:

1. gathering for worship at certain times, most often weekends, but other days as well
2. literate and wide-ranging sources for our words
3. times set aside in our celebrations for heart to heart connection, singing, silence, ritual
4. thoughtful reflections on world, spirit, depth, and transition, and
5. stories, sermons, and talks of varying length.

Each congregation, each open circle of celebration, is unique as well.

When we enter any door that leads into our worship centers, we enter into distinct histories, styles, traditions, and practices not shared by other Unitarian Universalist communities. Such uniqueness is also our way.

We may differ, for example, on *where* we place announcements or the offering in the flow of service. Or we may question whether those are part of the service at all.

Sermons may be preached in their entirety at one time in the service, with readings from ancient and modern sources. Or they may be divided up into smaller talks with many voices.

The various styles of music and devotion among us differ too. A song sung every Sunday in one congregation may not be sung at all in another. A ritual candle that soothes one congregation does not work in another; a rich order with many readings and an unvarying set of opening words that date back decades will bring depth to one congregation, whereas in another community, form and function change with each passing season, and a deliberate simplicity of form is the received heritage.

Also, the theological language that grounds praise and wonder in one place may not be as engaging in another. A story or metaphor that lifts up one heart may block another's.

Thus, the creation of worship among us calls for our deepest mindfulness, our embracing heart, and an adventuresome spirit. The Celebration of Life shares the remarkable capacities of any other art form. It can soothe and ground us, or startle and shake us. It can shape us into a community of shared mourning and joy, or challenge us to respond to injustices in ways we had not imagined before. Worship can raise questions and bless diverse answers. Best of all, it can mobilize us to face the outrages, shallowness, and violence of our era from within a powerful circle of hope, shared grief, depth, and courage. Good worship, in whatever form, can free us to become the people we often imagine ourselves to be at our best.

These readings are just that, resources to help in creating good worship. They will prove useful in a variety of ways and inspire different forms in our various communities.

In the hands of the people, readings may be used straightforwardly, certainly.

Opening and closing words and the various affirmations work well with unison reading or, in some clear cases, antiphonal voices.

But the same readings may be divided into to two or more singular voices in the pulpit, which will offer a different tone or stress to the various images. Repeated lines in litanies could be chanted or sung, with music supplied by various members of our communities who are skillful composers, especially members of the Unitarian Universalist Musicians Network. Some folks (only a few!) can improvise simple musical lines right on the spot, which can enrich the spirit of the moment.

Responses can be divided into the voices of the various generations, or the various genders, or even just higher voices and lower voices. Readings may not be useful in their whole form, and only a smaller section may work best on any particular day.

Some readings benefit from repetition at several times in the Celebration, so that in the words of the poet, "we can know the place for the first time."

Readings can be combined or gathered into groups. Or verses of readings can be interspersed with verses of songs that complement the ideas or intensify the feelings. Movement and dance can work with many of these readings, read dramatically, with the images reimagined by gesture and choreography.

Smaller readings can be broken down into individual sentences which might be used throughout the service, one at a time.

Readings in Spanish can be read by those who know Spanish, now many in our communities. Not every reading needs to be read by everyone.

And some folks do not relate to unison reading at all, but they might indeed benefit from reading the various options in private, keeping the book by the bedside, for example, as many did with the hymnbook *Singing the Living Tradition*. The readings in this book are certainly a supplement to the resources in that book.

This is a book which can nourish the spirit in every single one of our unique congregations and open circles of celebration, when used with thoughtfulness, creativity, and even some daring by worship leaders both ordained and lay.

As time goes on, the great spread of online resources will enable people to communicate with others, and share the ways they have found within this compendium to deepen and excite the worship lives in our communities.

Let the present generation build on the past generations of progressive worship practice to serve the visions, demands, and transformations of this present age.

Suggested Hymn Pairings

A Note on Multicultural Readings

With humility and courage born of our history, we are called as Unitarian Universalists to build the Beloved Community, where all souls are welcome as blessings, and the human family lives whole and reconciled.

LEADERSHIP COUNCIL OF THE UNITARIAN UNIVERSALIST ASSOCIATION OF CONGREGATIONS, OCTOBER 2008

One of the great strengths of Unitarian Universalism, embodied in our six Sources, is our belief that spiritual wisdom speaks in many voices. This understanding is the key to welcoming all souls into our faith communities as blessings. Each new person we encounter has something to teach us. Values such as love, peace, compassion, and justice are expressed in every culture and tradition all over the world, in beautifully and powerfully different ways. Taken together, these expressions illuminate the various facets of these ideas, giving them nuance and depth. But only if we allow them to.

Looking for commonalities is the relatively easy part of forming a multicultural community. True multiculturalism, however, means being humble and brave enough to explore our different perspectives, experiences, traditions, and values while staying in relationship. It means bringing our whole selves to the table and inviting others to do the same, not just the parts that "fit in." It means being willing to be changed.

None of us feels welcomed as a blessing if we are asked to leave parts of ourselves behind, if we are constantly asked to translate our beliefs, perspectives, and spiritual questions into the language and frame of reference of the majority. We do not feel that we are recognized for the gifts we have to offer if our interactions and relationships leave no room for mutual transformation.

Learning from and about each other helps us practice true hospitality. When we share our cultural traditions with one another in worship, we can offer this welcoming message: "We value your rich tradition and worldview so much that we are committed to learning about it."

Often readings carry cultural resonances and meanings that extend beyond the words alone. If you use these readings in worship, in religious education, in small group ministry (and I hope you will), I encourage you to consider it part of your standard preparation to research some of their context. Learn and share as much as you can about the authors or speakers, their stories, their cultural and historical contexts, and the significance attached to what they've said or written.

If you use the Internet for your research, pay particular attention to websites and online books developed or published by cultural organizations and academic institutions. Personal websites are not reliable.

Once you learn more about a reading from a cultural tradition different from your own, you may become aware of its deeper meaning within its own context. For example, consider the following reading by Mohandas K. Gandhi:

> Non-violence is like radium in its action. An infinitesimal quantity of it embedded in a malignant growth acts continuously, silently and cease-lessly till it has transformed the whole mass of the diseased tissue into a healthy one. Similarly, even a little of true non-violence acts in a silent, subtle, unseen way and leavens the whole society.

Most people know the rough outline of Gandhi's story and that he is associated with the ethic of non-violence. But how many of us who are not Hindu, Buddhist, or Jain fully understand the implications of *ahimsa*, the sacred vow that was the foundation of Gandhi's activism? The depth and nuance of *ahimsa* cannot be conveyed by the English word *nonviolence*. With a brief Internet search, you can learn about Gandhi's understanding of *ahimsa*, congruencies and differences between *ahimsa* and Unitarian Universalist affirmations of the worth and dignity of every person and the interdependent web, Gandhi's legacy for activists Albert Schweitzer and Martin Luther King, Jr., and explanations of *ahimsa* as the philosophical basis for Hindu practices like yoga and vegetarianism that have become popular in the West.

Unitarian Universalists are a people engaged in the perpetual search for truth and meaning. What any one of us knows and has experienced is only one piece of the truth. Let us open ourselves to what we can learn from each other, as well as from those we have yet to meet.

Awe, Mystery, and Spirit

1

You, darkness, of whom I am born—

I love you more than the flame
that limits the world
to the circle it illumines
and excludes all the rest.

But the dark embraces everything:
shapes and shadows, creatures and me,
people and nations—just as they are.

It lets me imagine
a great presence stirring beside me.

I believe in the night.

> RAINER MARIA RILKE,
> TRANSLATED BY ANITA BARROWS
> AND JOANNA MACY

2

Give us the child who lives within . . .

*Give us a child's eyes, that we may
receive the beauty and freshness of
this day like a sunrise;*

Give us a child's ears, that we may
hear the music of mythical times;

*Give us a child's heart, that we may
be filled with wonder and delight;*

Give us a child's faith, that we may
be cured of our cynicism;

*Give us the spirit of the child, who is
not afraid to need; who is not afraid
to love.*

Amen.

> SARAH YORK, ADAPTED

3

You ask me how to pray to someone
  who is not.
All I know is that prayer constructs
  a velvet bridge
And walking it we are aloft, as on a
  springboard,
Above landscapes the color of ripe
  gold
Transformed by a magic stopping
  of the sun.
That bridge leads to the shore of
  Reversal
Where everything is just opposite
  and the word *is*
Unveils a meaning we hardly
  envisioned.
Notice: I say we; there, every one,
  separately,
Feels compassion for others entangled
  in the flesh
And knows that if there is no other
  shore
They will walk that aerial bridge all
  the same.

> CZESŁAW MILOSZ,
> TRANSLATED BY ROBERT HASS

4

We touch the floor

*to remember that wherever we bring
our best self is holy ground.*

We reach for the sky

*to remember that we are a part of a
mystery much bigger than ourselves.*

We hold hands

*to remember that we need one another
and are part of one human family.*

We join voices

*to remember that we each have a gift to
offer the world
and to use in making the world a better
place.*

LISA FRIEDMAN

5

Again the wind
flakes gold leaf from the trees
and the painting darkens—
as if a thousand penitents
kissed an icon
till it thinned
back to bare wood,
without diminishment.

JANE HIRSHFIELD

6

The hour is striking so close above me,
so clear and sharp,
that all my senses ring with it.
I feel it now: there's a power in me
to grasp and give shape to my world.

I know that nothing has ever been real
without my beholding it.
All becoming has needed me.
My looking ripens things
and they come toward me, to meet
and be met.

RAINER MARIA RILKE,
TRANSLATED BY ANITA BARROWS
AND JOANNA MACY

7

To be of the Earth is to know

the restlessness of being a seed

the darkness of being planted

the struggle toward the light

the pain of growth into the light

the joy of bursting and bearing fruit

the love of being food for someone

the scattering of your seeds

the decay of the seasons

the mystery of death

and the miracle of birth.

JOHN SOOS, ADAPTED

8

The lower leaves of the trees
Tangle the sunset in dusk.
Awe spreads with
The summer twilight.

Sone No Yoshitada,
translated by Kenneth Rexroth

9

We have not forgotten;
in nature we seek you
in the whisper of wind
in the new green wood

Your presence is near

We have not lost hope;
in the dust of the desert
in the rush of the wave
in the rise of the mountain

Your presence is near

We remember the cycle;
in the promise of blossoms
in the dying leaves
in the bare branches
your presence is near

Julianne Lepp

10

Now the autumn shudders
    In the rose's root.
Far and wide the ladders
    Lean among the fruit.

*Now the autumn clambers
    Up the trellised frame,
And the rose remembers
    The dust from which it came.*

Brighter than the blossom
    On the rose's bough
Sits the wizened orange,
    Bitter berry now;

*Beauty never slumbers;
    All is in her name;
But the rose remembers
    The dust from which it came.*

Edna St. Vincent Millay, adapted

11

What is praised is one,

*so the praise is one too,
many jugs being poured
into a huge basin.*

All religions, all this singing, one song.

*The differences are just illusion and
    vanity.*

Sunlight looks slightly different on
    this wall than it does on that wall
    and a lot different on this other
    one, but it is still one light.

*We have borrowed these clothes, these
time-and-space personalities,
from a light, and when we praise, we
    pour them back in.*

Jalal al-Din Rumi,
translated by Coleman Barks,
adapted

12

Between the poles of the conscious
   and the unconscious,
there has the mind made a swing:

Thereon hang all beings and all worlds,
and that swing never ceases its sway.

Millions of beings are there: the sun
   and the moon
in their courses are there;

Millions of ages pass, and the swing
   goes on.

All swing! the sky and the earth and
   the air and the water. . . .

      KABIR, TRANSLATED BY
      RABINDRANATH TAGORE, ADAPTED

13

There is a mystery within me,
and try as I may,
I cannot come to the end of it.
It teaches me reverence
for the unfathomable wonder at my
   core.
Hidden One, You alone
know the secret
within the secret within me,
for are You not that secret?

      CHAIM STERN

14

We receive fragments of holiness,
glimpses of eternity,
brief moments of insight.

Let us gather them up
for the precious gifts that they are
and, renewed by their grace,
move boldly into the unknown.

      SARAH YORK

15

No matter what they tell you,
let it be about joy,
let it be about the sacred!
Self surviving—no, thriving—
shining its way to the knowledge
   within.
Let it be about blooming,
the unfolding of the universe
   through you,
because the story of you begins
fifteen billion years ago
with that first flash of being.

      NITA PENFOLD

16

I have been looking for the words
   that come
before words: the ones older than
   silence,
the ones not mine, that can't be
   found by thought—
the ones that hold the beginning of
   the world
and are never used up, which arrive
   loaned,
and make me weep.

      NANCY SHAFFER

17

As swimmers dare
to lie face to the sky
and water bears them,
as hawks rest upon air
and air sustains them,
so would I learn to attain
freefall, and float
into Creator Spirit's deep embrace,
knowing no effort earns
that all-surrounding grace.

DENISE LEVERTOV

18

This singing art is sea foam.

*The graceful movements come from a
  pearl*
somewhere on the ocean floor.

Poems reach up like spindrift and
  the edge
of driftwood along the beach,
  wanting!

They derive
from a slow and powerful root
that we can't see.

Stop the words now.
Open the window in the centre of
  your chest,
and let the spirits fly in and out.

JALAL AL-DIN RUMI,
TRANSLATED BY
COLEMAN BARKS, ADAPTED

19

How does one address a mystery?

Cautiously—let us go cautiously,
  then, to the end of our certainty,
  to the boundary of all we know,
  to the rim of uncertainty, to the
  perimeter of the unknown which
  surrounds us.

Reverently—let us go with a sense
  of awe, a feeling of approaching
  the powerful holy whose lightning
  slashes the sky, whose persistence
  splits concrete with green sprouts,
  whose miracles are present in every
  place and moment.

Hopefully—out of our need for
  wholeness in our own lives, the
  reconciliation of mind and heart,
  the conjunction of reason and
  passion, the intersection of the
  timeless with time.

Quietly—for no words will explain
  the inarticulate or summon the
  presence that is always present even
  in our absence.

But what shall I say?

Anything—any anger, any hope,
  any fear, any joy, any request, any
  word that comes from the depth
  of being addressed to Being itself—
  or, perhaps, nothing, no complaint,
  no request, no entreaty, no
  thanksgiving, no praise, no blame,
  no pretense of knowing or of not
  knowing.

Simply be in the intimate presence of
mystery, unashamed—unadorned—
unafraid.

And at the end say—Amen.

GORDON B. MCKEEMAN

20

A planet is born, a spark ignites,
something completely new comes
into being;

*we give thanks for the mystery and
miracle of life.*

A waterfall descends, a rainbow arcs
through the sky, the ocean opens
to an endless horizon;

*we give thanks for the mystery and
miracle of beauty.*

The stars pierce our hearts, peace
envelops us, we are blessed;

*we give thanks for the mystery and
miracle of wonder.*

In the midst of pain, we find our
way to hope and restoration;

*we give thanks for the mystery and
miracle of healing.*

In the midst of fear, we do what is
right and speak our truth in faith;

*We give thanks for the mystery and
miracle of courage.*

In our aloneness we see someone in
greater need and offer ourselves to
them;

*We give thanks for the mystery and
miracle of compassion.*

We gather in community, in
relationship, in friendship, and
cherish each other;

*We give thanks for the mystery and
miracle of love.*

AMANDA UDIS-KESSLER

21

God be in my head,

and in my understanding;

God be in my eyes, and in my
looking;

*God be in my mouth, and in my
speaking;*

God be in my heart, and in my
thinking;

*God be at mine end, and at my
departing.*

Amen.

SARUM PRIMER, ADAPTED

Beloved Community

22

We pause this morning
from the chaos of the world
to reclaim the beauty within these
walls
that carry us through our week,

We lift this community onto our
shoulders
with pride and grace-filled expectations
for our children
and our children's children.

Marta I. Valentín

23

Spirit of Life,

You speak to us from the East and the
West
You speak to us from the North and
the South
You call to us from the depths of our
being
We respond with enthusiasm and
fervor
We cry out from Manila to Maui
We shout from Alaska to Alabama
We proclaim your wondrous love
from the highest mountain to the
deepest ocean
Our voices must be heard. We shall
not be silent.
Our voices must be heard.

Jonipher Kwong

24

Here in the refuge of this Sabbath
home
we turn our busy minds toward silence,
and our full hearts toward one another.

We move together through the mysteries:
the bright surprise of birth and the
shadowed questions of death.

In our slow walk between the two we
will be wounded,
and we will be showered with grace,
amazing, unending.

Even in our sorrows, we feel our lives
cradled in holiness we cannot
comprehend.

And though we each walk within a
vast loneliness,
the promise we offer here is that we
do not walk alone.
This is a holy place in which we
gather—
the light of the earth brought in and
held,
touched then by our answering light:

the flame on a chalice,
the flicker of a candle,
the lamps of our open faces brought near.
In this place of silence and celebration,
solemnity and music,
we make a sanctuary and name our
home.

Kathleen McTigue, adapted

25

Into this home we bring our hunger
   for awakening.
We bring compassionate hearts,
and a will toward justice.
Into this home we bring the courage
   to walk on
after hard losses.
Into this home we bring our joy,
and gratitude for ordinary blessings.
By our gathering we bless this place.
In its shelter we know ourselves
   blessed.

KATHLEEN MCTIGUE

If we are steady and composed,
If we feel completely lost,
If we don't know what we are feeling,

this community has a place for us . . .
here, we matter,
and we are loved.

If you are steady and poised,
If you feel completely lost,
If you don't know what you feel,
this community has a place for us . . .
we matter,
we are loved.

WENDY BARTEL AND
LYNN GARDNER

26

From our separate joys and struggles,
   we come here
to find the peace of balance,
to find the blessing of restlessness.

All are welcome

to follow, to lead
to teach, to learn
All are welcome

to join in the dance
to catch our breath. . . .
All are welcome

to give generously
to receive gratefully.

All are welcome.

27

Come burdened
Come savvy
Come aging
Come discouraged
Come wanting
Come full
Come longing
Come drifting
Come!

KATHERINE HAWKERSELF,
ADAPTED

28

1. In this familiar place, listen:
to the sounds of breathing,
    creaking chairs,
shuffling feet, clearing throats,
    and sighing all around
Know that each breath,
    movement, the glance
meant for you or intercepted
holds a life within it.

2. These are signs
that we choose to be in this
    company
have things to say to each other
things not yet said but in each
    other's presence still
trembling behind our hearts' doors
these doors closed but unlocked
each silent thing waiting
on the threshold between
    unknowing and knowing,
between being hidden and being
    known.

TOGETHER: Listen: rejoice. And say
Amen.

BARBARA J. PESCAN, ADAPTED

29

READER 1: You who are broken-
    hearted,
who woke today with the winds
    of despair
whistling through your mind,
come in.

READER 2: You who are brave but
    wounded,
limping through life and hurting
    with every step,
come in.

READER 1: You who are fearful, who
    live with shadows
hovering over your shoulders,
come in.

TOGETHER: This place is sanctuary,
    and it is for you.

READER 1: You who are filled with
    happiness,
whose abundance overflows,
come in.

READER 2: You who walk through
    your world
with lightness and grace,
who awoke this morning with
    strength and hope,
you who have everything to give,
come in.

READER 1: This place is your calling,
    a riverbank to channel
the sweet waters of your life,

READER 2: the place where you are
    called by the world's need.
Here we offer in love.

READER 1: Here we receive in
    gratitude.
Here we make a circle from the
    great gifts
of breath, attention and purpose.

TOGETHER: Come in.

KATHLEEN McTIGUE, ADAPTED

30

Leave aside the little thoughts
that distract you,
for this place, like all places, is a holy
    place, and
now, like all times, is a holy time.
Join with
this community of seekers,
and together, let us find.

JOHN GIBB MILLSPAUGH

31

As we enter this shared, sacred space,
let us renew both our commitment
    and our covenant:

There are those among us who have
    endured a loss in the past week.
*May their hope be uplifted again in
    this community of faith.*
May they find renewed strength.
There are those among us who have
    wrestled with questions that seem
    to have no answer this past week.
*May they find sanctuary in this
    community of faith.*
There are those among us who have
    cherished an unexpected joy in
    the past week;
May their gladness be celebrated.
As we commit to continue our free
    and responsible search for Truth,
*may we covenant to honor the many
    paths that have led us to this
    community.*

MARTHA KIRBY CAPO

32

Let us take a moment to relax and
catch our breath. Let us bring our
focus here, to this room, to this
group of people and to this moment.
We bring a myriad of talents, ideas,
needs, and styles. Yet within this
diversity, there is a common bond
between us. We love this fellowship,
and we are willing to work together
to improve and strengthen this
community of ours and our lives.

BERNADETTE R. BURNS

33

We gather as leaders, as servants.

We gather as ears, as voices.

We gather as memory, as hope.

We gather as family, as pilgrims.

We gather as faithful, as skeptics.

We gather as objects, as subjects.

We gather as wisdom, as folly.

We gather as action, as reflection.

We gather as many, as one.

ALL: As we are, we shall be.
    As we serve,
    so shall we lead.

PATRICK MURFIN, ADAPTED

34

And so I say ours is a story of faith
   and hope and love.
I say it is our need for one another
   that binds us together,
that brings us laughing and limping
   into relationships
and keeps us at it when we otherwise
   might despair at the fix we are in.

I say it is the holy we need, the
   eternal beyond our comprehension,
and one place we can find it is here,
   working and worshipping together.

And I say there is a transcendent
   value worthy of our loyalty,
upon which we may set our hearts,
and its divine manifestation is love.

ELIZABETH TARBOX, ADAPTED

35

Community is the spirit, the guiding
   light of the tribe,
whereby people come together in
   order to fulfill a specific purpose,
to help others fulfill their purpose,
   and to take care of one another.

SOBONFU SOMÉ

36

We are all longing to go home to
   some place
we have never been—a place, half-
   remembered, and half-envisioned

we can only catch glimpses of from
   time to time.
Community.
Somewhere, there are people to
   whom we can speak with passion
without having the words catch in
   our throats.
Somewhere a circle of hands
will open to receive us, eyes will light
   up as we enter, voices will celebrate
   with us whenever we come into
   our own power.
Community means strength
that joins our strength to do the work
   that needs to be done.
Arms to hold us when we falter.
A circle of healing.
A circle of friends.
Someplace where we can be free.

STARHAWK

37

For all of life
and gifts we hold sacred,

we raise our voices.

For all our relations
we will meet with compassion and
   grace,

we raise our voices.

For justice and peace
and the health of all the cycle of life,

we raise our voices.

For the celebration of all
who themselves can not, or may not,

we raise our voices.

For the rememberance of those
who have taught, lead, or inspired us,

we raise our voices.

For this moment in time that we are
granted
to share the wealth of each other's
presence,

we raise our voices.

For the power of our collective voice
and concerted action, with vision
and love

we raise our voices.

JIM SCOTT

38

Here in this place of peace, may we
find hope.
Here in this place of connection, may
we find life-giving community.
Here in this place of rest, let the
unrest of our hearts turn us toward
justice.
Here in this space made sacred by
memories of connection,
let us each feel ourselves part of the
new that grows from the old
in the spiraling unity of years.

LESLIE TAKAHASHI

39

None of our private worlds is big
enough for us to live a wholesome
life in.

*We need the wider world of joy and
wonder, of purpose and venture, of
toil and tears.*

What are we, any of us, but strangers
and sojourners
forlornly wandering through the
nighttime until we draw together
and find the meaning of our lives in
one another,
dissolving our fears in each other's
courage, making music together
and lighting torches to guide us
through the dark? We belong
together.

*Love is what we need. To love and to
be loved.*
*Let our hearts be open; and what we
would receive from others, let us give.*
*For what is given still remains to bless
the giver—when the gift is love.*

A. POWELL DAVIES, ADAPTED

40

Why community? To remember . . .

That one is not a whole number
That we need both roots and wings
That strength comes from relationship
and mutuality
That we know life in and through one
another

PAMELA RUMANCIK

41

Each of us brings a separate truth
here.

*We bring the truth of our own life,
our own story.*

We don't come as empty vessels but
as full people,
each with our own story and our
own truth.
*We seek to add to our truths and add
to our stories.
This room is rich with truth, rich
with experience.*

All manner of people are here:
needy
joyful
frightened
anxious
bored

We all bring our truth with us.

May we all recognize the truth
and the story in other lives than
our own.
May we hear and honor the truths
that we all bring as we gather
together.

Together we have truths.

Together we have a story.

Together we are a community.

PENNY HACKETT-EVANS

42

Spirit of life,
be present with us this hour.

*Join us today as we gather in a wider
search for truth and purpose.*

In this quest, may we greet one
another
with open hearts and minds;

*may we inspire each other to consider
new questions
and seek deeper meaning;*

may we cultivate wisdom and
compassion.

*Let all who enter this sanctuary see a
welcome face,
hear a kind word, and find comfort
in this community.*

And may all that is done and said
here today
be in service to love and justice.

KATHY HUFF

Courage and Call to Action

43

We are living in the greatest
  revolution in history—
a huge spontaneous upheaval of the
  entire human race:
not a revolution planned and carried
  out
by any particular party, race, or
  nation,
but a deep elemental boiling over
of all the inner contradictions that
  have ever been,
a revelation of the chaotic forces
  inside everybody.
This is not something we have
  chosen,
nor is it something we are free to
  avoid.

THOMAS MERTON, ADAPTED

44

SOLO VOICE: Where are we to go
  when this is through?
  We are the war-born. What are we
  to do?

LEFT: Where are we to go when this
  is done?
  Will we slip into old, accustomed
  ways,
  finding remembered notches, one
  by one?
  Thrashing a hapless way through
  quickening haze?

RIGHT: Who is to know us when the
  end has come?
  Old friends and families, but
  could we be
  strange to the sight and stricken
  dumb
  at visions of some pulsing
  memory?

LEFT: Who will love us for what we
  used to be
  who now are what we are, bitter
  or cold?

RIGHT: Who is to nurse us with swift
  subtlety
  back to the warm and feeling
  human fold?

SOLO VOICE: Where are we to go
  when this is through?
  We are the war-born. What are we
  to do?

ALFRED A. DUCKETT, ADAPTED

45

If I am not for myself, who will be
  for me?
And if I am only for myself, what
  am I?
And if not now, when?

HILLEL

46

I have walked that long road to
   freedom.
I have tried not to falter;
I have made missteps along the way.
But I have discovered the secret that
after climbing a great hill, one only
   finds
that there are many more hills to
   climb.
I have taken a moment here to rest,
To steal a view of the glorious vista
that surrounds me, to look back
on the distance I have come.
But I can rest only for a moment,
for with freedom come
   responsibilities,
and I dare not linger, for my long walk
is not yet ended.

NELSON MANDELA

47

Your gifts
whatever you discover them to be
can be used to bless or curse the
   world.

The mind's power,

The strength of the hands,

The reaches of the heart,

the gift of speaking, listening,
   imagining, seeing, waiting

*Any of these can serve to feed the
   hungry,*

bind up wounds,

welcome the stranger,

praise what is sacred,

*do the work of justice
or offer love.
Any of these can draw down the
   prison door,*

hoard bread,

abandon the poor,

obscure what is holy,

comply with injustice

or withhold love.

You must answer this question:
What will you do with your gifts?

REBECCA ANN PARKER, ADAPTED

48

We are here to face the truth, about
   ourselves, about this faith we love,
   and the ways it presently serves
   others and the world,

*As well as to open ourselves to ways it
   can better, and more joyfully, reflect
   our potential and core values.*

*We want to know the ways we are
   bound to one another, as well as to
   larger religious movements normally
   beyond our sight and vision*

We say we are open and diverse

*Yet it is too easy to feel stuck in old
paths and stubborn habits reflecting
not so much tradition as our comfort.*

We want to answer the call to service,
to a world that needs our message,
our hope, our revived energy—

*We are gathered to learn, to unlearn, to
hear, and to move forward. Amen.*

STEPHEN KENDRICK

49

LEFT: Like never before, the presence
of the other in all of its beauty,
fragility, dignity, and need is
demanding our answers. . . .

RIGHT: These questions, if entertained,
might demand that we change
our theologies, liturgies, and
practices.

LEFT: The bondage of certainty can
supplant the freedom of faith
and make it impossible for us
to say:

ALL: We don't know.
We apologize.
We want to change.
What can we do to make things
right? . . .

RIGHT: The heart of a religion that
will bless the world
is going to beat at its edges.

SAMIR SELMANOVIC, ADAPTED

50

We must shine.

We must shine now.

This is the goal toward which we
stretch,

step by step,

in our own time, at our own pace.

*As our beauty unfolds, and our hearts
open,*

we become gentler and more
compassionate,

*yet brighter, more empowered, and
fearless.*

We have been holding on, holding
back,

*playing small, hiding our light under
a bushel.*

Enough of that.

It is time to let go.

We are needed now, all of us.

All of us together,

ALL: All those who feel a calling
to be who we are to the fullest,
make a difference, to give it all
we got.

CHRISTIAN DE LA HUERTA,
ADAPTED

51

Source of Life,
We have been given time to measure
our days.

*What are we to make of these times,
these times in which we live and love
and have our being?*

The road of history has been long, full
of both hope and disappointment.

*There have been wars and rumors of
wars,*

violence and exploitation, hunger and
homelessness, and destruction.

*We know that we cannot continue to
live in the old way. We must make
a change, seek a new way. A way
leading toward peace with justice
and a healthy planet.*

Creative Spirit: You have given a
vision for the good, and we yearn
for a new way. But where are we to
find the courage to begin to work
for this new beginning? We wonder
what is required of us.

*We think of the prophets, women and
men who gave voice to unpopular
opinion, who made personal sacrifices,
sometimes their lives, for the sake of
justice.*

May we be inspired and renewed by
the courage of these witnesses.
Let them empower us as we work for
this vision.

So may it be. Amen.

CLYDE GRUBBS

52

A time like this demands great
leaders;

*Leaders whom the lust of office does
not kill;*

Leaders whom the spoils of life
cannot buy;

*Leaders who possess opinions and
a will;*

Leaders who have honor;

Leaders who will not lie;

Leaders who can stand before a
demagogue
and damn . . . treacherous flatteries
without winking!

*Tall leaders, sun crowned, who live
above the fog
in public duty and private thinking.*

MARTIN LUTHER KING JR., ADAPTED

53

Our time together is finished
but our work is not done.

*May our spirits be renewed
and our resolve strengthened
as we meet the challenges
of the week to come.*

This chalice flame is extinguished
until we ignite it again

with the spark of our communion.

MARTHA KIRBY CAPO

54

I confess my own inner confusion as
    I look out upon the world.
There is food for all—

many are hungry.

There are clothes enough for all—

many are in rags.

There is room enough for all—

many are crowded.

There are none who want war—

preparations for conflict abound.

Let Thy light burn in me that I may,
    from this moment on, take
    effective steps within my own
    powers, to live up to the light and
    courageously to pay for the kind of
    world I so deeply desire.

HOWARD THURMAN, ADAPTED

55

So often words fail us
And we do not know to whom or
    what to pray.

We ask for legs that can walk for peace,
Arms that can work for justice,
Voices that can speak with love,
Hands that can soothe a feverish brow.

By our actions and voices
May our prayers be sent.

Shalom. Salaam. Om. Amen.

JANE ELLEN MAULDIN, ADAPTED

56

Spirit of Life,

May our fumbling tongues be blessed
so that chatter becomes prayer
and prayer becomes concerted action.

May our restless minds be blessed
so that insight becomes will
and will becomes effective action.

May our anxious hearts be blessed
so that longing becomes love
and love guides our every action.

BARNABY FEDER

57

Into our world we entrust our spirits:
May the strength we have gained in
    this communal hour
Sustain us as we resume the work
    that is at hand.

MARTHA KIRBY CAPO

58

Though much is taken, much abides;
    and though
We are not now that strength which
    in old days
Moved earth and heaven, that which
    we are, we are;
One equal temper of heroic hearts,
Made weak by time and fate, but
    strong in will
To strive, to seek, to find, and not to
    yield.

ALFRED, LORD TENNYSON

59

God grant that ministers, and lay
    leaders, and civic leaders,
. . . and professional people all over
    the nation
will rise up and use the talents and the
    finances that God has given them,
and lead the people on toward the
    promised land of freedom
with rational, calm, nonviolent means.

MARTIN LUTHER KING JR.

60

You work that you may keep pace
    with the earth and the soul of the
    earth.

*For to be idle is to become a stranger
    unto the seasons, and to step out of
    life's procession, that marches in
    majesty and proud submission
    towards the infinite.*

When you work you are a flute
    through whose heart the whispering
    of the hours turns to music.

*Which of you would be a reed, dumb
    and silent, when all else sings together
    in unison?*

Always you have been told that work
    is a curse and labour a misfortune.

*But I say to you that when you work
    you fulfil a part of earth's furthest
    dream, assigned to you when that
    dream was born,*

And in keeping yourself with labour
    you are in truth loving life,

*And to love life through labour is to be
    intimate with life's inmost secret.*

KAHLIL GIBRAN, ADAPTED

61

Oh sun, moon, stars, our other
    relatives peering at us from the
    inside of god's house, walk with us
    as we climb . . . naked but for the
    stories we have of each other. Keep
    us from giving up in this land of
    nightmares which is also the land
    of miracles.

*We sing our song which we've been
    promised has no beginning or end.*

JOY HARJO, ADAPTED

62

A Presence
summoned hearts from all ages,
    whole, holy.
They answered the summons humbly,
to find Light.
They saw, tasted, and lived the sparks,
and proclaimed brilliance to the
    shadows.

*They did not brag of prosperity,
nor tout their shining intellect,
nor use some mighty gift of power.
Simplicity of heart was their only gift.*

Now the summons sounds again.
A still small voice for singular people,
whose honest hearts opened,
filled with love for neighbors, which
 is love for God.

Do we hear the still small voice?
Can we respond with our lives?
Will we join the gathering ranks
to reflect the Light of Presence into a
 confused world?

ARYANTO NUGROHO

63

We have tomorrow
Bright before us
Like a flame.

Yesterday
A night-gone thing,
A sun-down name.

And dawn-today
Broad arch above the road we came.

We march!

LANGSTON HUGHES, ADAPTED

64

For the longing that told you it was
 time for a change,

we give you our blessings.

For the courage it took to answer
 the call,

we give you our blessings.

For the choices already made, and
 for the daily choices that will shape
 the life ahead of you,

we give you our blessings.

For the communities that have shown
 you who you are and the new
 communities waiting to discover
 you in your new ventures,

we give you our blessings.

For the great mystery of what lies
 ahead,

We give you our blessings and our love.

May you see something of beauty
 along the way,
touch hands with those you love,
and give more than you get.

JILL ANN TERWILLIGER

Grace

65

I hereby forgive all who have hurt me,

all who have wronged me,

whether deliberately or inadvertently,

whether by word or by deed.

May no one be punished on my
  account.

*As I forgive and pardon those who
  have wronged me,*

may those whom I have harmed
  forgive me,

*whether I acted deliberately or
  inadvertently,*

whether by word or by deed.

GATES OF REPENTANCE, ADAPTED

66

Life is the only way
to get covered in leaves,
catch your breath on the sand,
rise on wings;

to be a dog,
or stroke its warm fur;

to tell pain
from everything it's not;

to squeeze inside events,
dawdle in views,
to seek the least of all possible mistakes.

An extraordinary chance
to remember for a moment
a conversation held
with the lamp switched off.

And if only once,
to stumble on a stone,
end up drenched in one downpour or
  another,

mislay your keys in the grass;
and to follow a spark on the wind
  with your eyes;

and to keep on not knowing
something important.

WISŁAWA SZYMBORSKA, ADAPTED

67

We return again and again to the
  season of forgiveness
and each time we come, we come
  bearing gifts—

a grudge to relinquish,

a hatred to extinguish,

a hope that has bloated and distorted,

a glancing word that has wounded.
Each time we walk the road towards
  forgiveness,
we mutter that we have been here
  before.

21

When will we remember that
forgiveness is not so much an act
as an attitude,
not so much a duty as a love we give
ourselves
as part of the ever-unfolding new
beginning?

LESLIE TAKAHASHI

68

Every day is a god,

each day is a god,

and holiness holds forth in time.

I worship each god,

I praise each day splintered down,
and wrapped in time like a husk,

a husk of many colors spreading,
at dawn fast over the mountains split.

ANNIE DILLARD, ADAPTED

69

Whatever happens. Whatever
what is is is what
I want. Only that. But that.

GALWAY KINNELL

70

Much of ministry
 is a benediction
A speaking well of
 each other and the world
A speaking well of what we value:

honesty
love
forgiveness
trust

A speaking well of our efforts
A speaking well of our dreams

This is how we celebrate life:
through speaking well of it,
living the benediction
and becoming as a word well-spoken.

SUSAN MANKER-SEALE

71

Leaves don't fall. They descend.

Longing for earth, they come winging.
In their time they'll come again.

For leaves don't fall. They descend.

On the branches they will be again,
Green and fragrant, cradle-swinging,

For leaves don't fall. They descend.

Longing for earth, they come winging.

MALKA HEIFETZ TUSSMAN,
TRANSLATED BY
MARCIA FALK, ADAPTED

72

I hold the splendid daylight in my
    hands
Inwardly grateful for a lovely day.

Thank you life.

Daylight like a fine fan spread from
    my hands

Daylight like scarlet poinsettia

Daylight like yellow cassia flowers

Daylight like clean water

Daylight like green cacti

*Daylight like sea sparkling with white
    horses*

Daylight like sunstrained blue sky

Daylight like tropic hills

Daylight like a sacrament in my
    hands.

Amen.

GEORGE CAMPBELL, ADAPTED

73

Halleluia, Halleluia, Halleluia!

LEADER: Praise be to the spirit of all
    life

LEFT: To the machinery—
RIGHT: and to the momentum
LEFT: to the brick—
RIGHT: and to the soaring arch
LEFT: to the sanctuary—

RIGHT: and to the journey

LEADER: In wild unaccountable life,
    and the resilient seed

LEFT: To solemn gravity—
RIGHT: and to the uplifting wind
LEFT: to the habitual sun—
RIGHT: and capricious rain
LEFT: to the composition—
RIGHT: and the improvisation

LEADER: In the science and the art

LEFT: To the mathematics—
RIGHT: and as well, the music
LEFT: to the equation—
RIGHT: and as well, the poem
LEFT: to the prescription—
RIGHT: and as well, the dance

LEADER: In the tool and the artisan

LEFT: To the pallete—
RIGHT: and to the vision
LEFT: to the wisdom—
RIGHT: and to the faith
LEFT: to the lesson—
RIGHT: and to the dream

Halleluia, Halleluia, Halleluia!

JIM SCOTT

74

For the joyful,
may jubilant songs
echo in our hearts
well beyond fading memories.

For the sorrowful,
may gentle songs of solace
bring lasting healing
to our hearts and minds.

For the angry,
may we join our voices together
in songs of protest and hope.

For the mindful,
may we sing the praises
of Earth's beauty
and honor the unique songs of all
    beings.

For all of us here in our community,
    and our world,
may we sing to the morning and
    evening stars
as they guide our journeys.

BERNADETTE R. BURNS

75

Will you ever bring a better gift for
    the world
than the breathing respect that you
    carry
wherever you go right now? Are you
    waiting
for time to show you some better
    thoughts?

When you turn around, starting here,
    lift this
new glimpse that you found; carry
    into evening
all that you want from this day. This
    interval you spent

reading or hearing this, keep it for
life—

What can anyone give you greater
    than now,
starting here, right in this room,
    when you turn around?

WILLIAM STAFFORD

76

May our ears
hear
what nobody
wants to hear.

May our eyes
see
what everyone
wants to hide.

May our mouths
speak
our true faces
and hearts.

May our arms
be branches
that give shade
and joy.

let us be a drizzle
a sudden storm
let us get wet
in the rain.

let us be the key

the hand the door

the kick the ball

the road

Let us arrive
as children
to this huge
playground—

the universe

FRANCISCO X. ALARCÓN, ADAPTED

77

Let the knowing speak
Let the oppressed tell of their sorrows,
Of their salt and boundless grief.
Since even the wise and the brave
Must wonder. . . .
Let those who can endure their
    doubts
Speak for the comfort of the weary
Who weep to know.

CHARLES ENOCH WHEELER

78

Only where love and need are one,
And the work is play for mortal
    stakes,
Is the deed ever really done
For Heaven and the future's sakes.

ROBERT FROST

79

Nature's first green is gold,
Her hardest hue to hold.
Her early leaf's a flower;
But only so an hour.
Then leaf subsides to leaf.
So Eden sank to grief,
So dawn goes down to day.
Nothing gold can stay.

ROBERT FROST

80

READER 1: Earth take away
    Make away sorrow,
    Bury the lark's bones
    Under the turf.
    Bury my grief.

READER 2: Black crow tear away
    Rend away sorrow,
    Talon and beak
    Pluck out the heart
    And the nerves of pain,
    Tear away grief.

READER 3: Sleep take away
    Make away sorrow,
    Take away the time,
    Fade away place,
    Carry me away
    From the world of my sorrow.

READER 4: Song sigh away
    Breathe away sorrow,
    Words tell away,
    Spell away sorrow,
    Charm away grief.

KATHLEEN RAINE, ADAPTED

81

There is an elemental love in the
   universe
by which name we know each other
and encourage ourselves to live.

*There is a silver river that connects
   everything
from which some part of us never
   leaves.*

There is a mercy making its way
up through the ocean of the earth
to the shores of our feet.

*There is a music so sweet it is almost
   unbearable
that is composed between the ear
and the heart which reminds us.*

There is a diamond-glint, a seed
   of longing
in ourselves that recognizes the
   potential
absence of gravity in another.

*There is part of us that
says it is never too late to be reborn
on the inbreath each morning.*

Somewhere there is a basket
that contains all of our failures.

*It is a big basket. It wants to know
what to do with these.
Mercy has no use for them.*

STEPHEN LEVINE, ADAPTED

82

We have a soul at times.
No one's got it non-stop,
for keeps.

*Day after day,
year after year
may pass without it.*

Sometimes
it will settle for awhile
only in childhood's fears and raptures.
Sometimes only in astonishment
that we are old. . . .

*For every thousand conversations
it participates in one,
if even that,
since it prefers silence.*

Just when our body goes from ache
   to pain,
it slips off-duty.
It's picky:
it doesn't like seeing us in crowds,
our hustling for a dubious advantage
and creaky machinations make it sick.

*Joy and sorrow
aren't two different feelings for it.
It attends us
only when the two are joined.*

WISŁAWA SZYMBORSKA,
TRANSLATED BY STANISLAW
BARANCZAK AND CLARE
CAVANAGH, ADAPTED

83

Heavenly Father, heavenly Mother,
Holy and blessed is your true name.
We pray for your reign of peace to
    come,
We pray that your good will be done,
Let heaven and earth become one.
Give us this day the bread we need,
Give it to those who have none.
Let forgiveness flow like a river
    between us,
From each one to each one to each
    one.
Lead us to holy innocence
Beyond the evil of our days—
Come swiftly Mother, Father, come.
For yours is the power and the glory
    and the mercy:
Forever your name is All in One.

        PARKER J. PALMER,
        INSPIRED BY MATTHEW 6:9–13

Hope

84

With faith to face our challenges,
with love that casts out fear,
with hope to trust tomorrow,
we accept this day as the gift it is:
    a reason for rejoicing.

GARY KOWALSKI

85

LEFT: In the first glimmers of
    morning,
    the world begins to takes shape.

RIGHT: First vague outlines, patterns
    of light and dark,
    then colors—dun branches of trees
    and withered winter grass.
    The brightening sky bathes a
    familiar landscape
    with a glow as it sleepily reveals
    itself.

ALL: Blessed morning!

LEFT: Oh, to have another day,
    to wake from whatever night
    thoughts dwell within,

RIGHT: to rise and have the world
    unfold before us,

LEFT: where the possible unwinds
    into the actual,

RIGHT: where dreams await their
    fulfilling,

ALL: where we meet, once again, to
    live into the hope that gathers us.
    Blessed morning!

MARK WARD

86

As chill winds blast the last autumn
    leaves from the trees,
we gather with new purpose.
In each other's company,
we find warmth against the approach
    of winter's cold.
We look to the bounty of harvest to
    sustain us while the earth sleeps,
and we attend again to the wider
    circles of relationship,
reminded of the connections on
    which we depend.
In each face,
some softening with age, some blooming
    into maturity,
we see the human story revealed,
the journey we each walk from mystery
    to mystery.
There is cause for gratitude:
for the love we share, even if
    imperfect and not always fully
    realized.
Every day of our journeys,
we are given new opportunities to
    accept and to give love.

MARK WARD

87

We light this chalice—

*not because we must but because
we may.*

We light this chalice—

*not because we have the truth
but because we each come bearing
and seeking many truths.*

We light this chalice—

*in connection across culture, distance,
class, and language.*

We light this chalice—
that our religion may be a beacon

of light, hope, and justice.

We light this chalice

to kindle our hearts and our minds.

Lois E. Van Leer

88

In times of darkness, we stumble
toward the tiny flame.
*In times of cold, we seek the warming
fire.*

In times of repression, we reach for
the lamp of truth.
*In times of loss, we pray for the
comforting light.*

In times of joy, we light a candle of
celebration.

ALL: Spirit of Life, as we kindle this
light, help us find what we need
this day.

Brian Kiely

89

Great ideas, it has been said,
come into the world as gently as
doves.

*Perhaps then, if we listen attentively,
we shall hear amid the uproar of
empires and nations,
a faint flutter of wings, the gentle
stirring of life and hope.*

Some will say that this hope lies in
a nation;
others, in a human being.

*I believe rather that it is awakened,
revived,
nourished by millions of solitary
individuals
whose deeds and works every day
negate frontiers
and the crudest implications of
history.*

As a result, there shines forth
fleetingly
the ever-threatened truth
that each and every person,
on the foundation of their own
sufferings and joys,
builds for them all.

Albert Camus, translated by
Justin O'Brien, adapted

90

I can feel the suffering of millions
and yet, if I look up into the heavens,
I think that it will all come right,
that this cruelty too will end,
and that peace and tranquillity will
    return again.
In the meantime,
I must uphold my ideals,
for perhaps the time will come
when I shall be able to carry them
    out.

ANNE FRANK

91

The leaves fall, fall as from afar,
Like distant gardens withered in the
    heavens;
They fall with slow and lingering
    descent.

And in the nights the heavy Earth,
    too, falls
From out the stars into the Solitude.

Thus all doth fall. This hand of mine
    must fall
And lo! the other one:—it is the law.
But there is One who holds this
    falling
Infinitely softly in His hands.

RAINER MARIA RILKE,
TRANSLATED BY JESSIE LAMONT

92

READER 1: Perhaps these thoughts
    of ours
    will never find an audience
Perhaps the mistaken road
    will end in a mistake
Perhaps the lamps we light one
    at a time
    will be blown out, one at a
    time
Perhaps the candles of our lives
    will gutter out
    without lighting a fire to
    warm us

READER 2: Perhaps when all the tears
    have been shed
    the earth will be more fertile
Perhaps when we sing praises to
    the sun
    the sun will praise us in return
Perhaps these heavy burdens
    will strengthen our philosophy
Perhaps when we weep for those
    in misery
    we must be silent about miseries
    of our own

ALL: Perhaps
Because of our irresistible sense
    of mission
We have no choice

SHU TING, TRANSLATED BY
CAROLYN KIZER, ADAPTED

93

Hope rises.

It rises from the heart of life, here and now, beating with joy and sorrow.

Hope longs.

It longs for good to be affirmed, for justice and love to prevail, for suffering to be alleviated, and for life to flourish in peace.

Hope remembers.

It remembers the dreams of those who have gone before and reaches for connection with them across the boundary of death.

Hope acts.

It acts to bless, to protest, and to repair.

JOHN A. BUEHRENS AND
REBECCA ANN PARKER, ADAPTED

94

Let our conversations with children
open them—and us
—to ever-wider circles of awareness.

Let them open up wider circles of spiritual life, spiritual joy, wider circles of faithful living.

Let them also give our children
strength and hope and meaning
for those times when they feel lonely
and we cannot be there for them,

when they feel pain because of the cruelties of the world;

when they feel guilt and shame and struggle for direction;
when they face dangers from which they need
more than human protection,
when they feel grief and rage
as well as awe and reverence.

Let us have conversations
that will ground them in faith, giving
them songs and stories and images
that make that faith accessible.

JEANNE HARRISON NIEUWEJAAR

95

Give me hunger,
O you gods that sit and give
The world its orders.
Give me hunger, pain and want,
Shut me out with shame and failure
From your doors of gold and fame,
Give me your shabbiest, weariest
hunger!

But leave me a little love,
A voice to speak to me in the day end,
A hand to touch me in the dark room
Breaking the long loneliness.
In the dusk of day-shapes
Blurring the sunset,
One little wandering, western star
Thrust out from the changing shores of shadow.
Let me go to the window,
Watch there the day-shapes of dusk
And wait and know the coming
Of a little love.

CARL SANDBURG, ADAPTED

96

This is a prayer for all the travelers.
For the ones who start out in beauty,
who fall from grace,
who step gingerly,
looking for the way back.
And for those who are born into the
margins,
who travel from one liminal space to
another,
crossing boundaries in search of
center.

This is a prayer for the ones whose
births
are a passing from darkness to
darkness,
who all their lives are drawn toward
the light,
and for those whose journeys
are a winding road that begins
and ends in the same place,
though only when the journey is
completed
do they finally know where they are.

For all the travelers, young and old,
aching and joyful,
weary and full of life;
the ones who are here, and the ones
who are not here;
the ones who are like you (and they're
all like you)
and the ones who are different (for
in some ways, we each travel
alone).

This is a prayer for traveling mercies,
And surefootedness,
for bread for your body and spirit,
for water,
for your safe arrival
and for everyone you see along the
way.

ANGELA HERRERA

97

Esta oración es para todos los viajeros.
Para los que comienzan en la belleza
y caen de la gracia,
quienes caminan tímidamente,
buscando la manera de volver.
Y para los que nacen en los márgenes,
viajando de un lugar liminal a otro, ⸌
cruzando fronteras
en busca del centro.

Es una oración para aquellos cuyo
nacimiento
es el paso de oscuridad a oscuridad,
aquellos que se sienten atraídos por
la luz,
y avanzan hacia ella.
Y para aquellos cuyas jornadas
son un camino sinuoso
que comienza y termina en el mismo
lugar,
aunque sólo al terminar,
sabrán por fin donde están.

Para todos los viajeros,
jóvenes y viejos,
dolientes y alegres,

cansados y llenos de vida;
los presentes y los ausentes,
los que son como tú (y todos son
    como tú)
y los que son distintos (porque de
    alguna manera
todos viajamos solos).

Esta es una oración por la misericordia,
para que andes con pie firme,
y visión clara;
por el pan para tu cuerpo y tu espíritu,
por el agua;
para que llegues seguro,
y para todos aquellos que encuentres
en el camino.

ANGELA HERRERA

98

We pause this hour to remember
those whom we have lost,
those whom we fear losing,
those from whom we are separated,
those to whom we would extend a
    helping hand,
a caring heart, the will to live.

We pause this hour also to hope
for life and good living,
for love and kind words,
for reconciliation,
for the support of family and friends,
for meaning in our struggle,
for wholeness.

May our memories and hope renew
    us for the days and nights to come.

M. SUSAN MILNOR

99

Spirit of Life and Love,
we live in a fragmented world that
    tempts us to despair.

*We would put it back together, piece
    by piece,*
if it were ours to choose.

But sometimes the fragments are
    enough.

In a world of cruelty,

*there is still power in every act of
    kindness.*

In a time of doubt,

there is still power in every act of hope.

In an age of division,

there is still power in every act of unity.

May we remember that sometimes
the fragments of meaning we make
are just the right size to hold in our
    hands.

LISA FRIEDMAN

100

As the kindling of this chalice calls
    us to community,

let there be light.

As the flame of this chalice reminds
    us of our values,

let there be light.

As the glow of this chalice encourages
us to hope,

let there be light.

Let there be light.

Maureen Killoran

101

To rescue our children we will have to
let them save us from the power we
embody:

*we will have to trust the very difference
that they forever personify.*

And we will have to allow them the
choice, without fear of death:
that they may come and do likewise

*or that they may come and that we will
follow them,
that a little child will lead us back to
the child we will always be,
vulnerable and wanting and hurting
for love and for beauty.*

June Jordan, adapted

102

Don't worry about saving these songs!
And if one of our instruments breaks,
it doesn't matter.

*We have fallen into the place
where everything is music.*

The strumming and the flute notes
rise into the atmosphere,
and even if the whole world's harp
should burn up, there will still be
hidden instruments playing.

*So the candle flickers and goes out.
We have a piece of flint, and a spark.*

Jalal al-Din Rumi,
translated by
Coleman Barks, adapted

103

LEFT SIDE: Once upon a time I was
Now I am
Some day I will become

RIGHT SIDE: Once there was
And now there is
Soon there will be
And some day there surely shall be

ALL: Once upon a time we were
Now we are
And some day (Hallelujah!) we
shall surely become

LEFT SIDE: Amen

RIGHT SIDE: Amen

Margaret Williams Braxton,
adapted

104

PARENTS: Our job with you has been
to fix the unfixable, to guide, to
mold, to expose you to beauty
and the wonder of the world.

YOUTH: Our job with you has been to bring you broken bones, tears from laughter, half-dead flowers, silent fears, amazing stories both true and fiction.

PARENTS: Our job with you has been to give you unconditional love, time to reflect, places to remember, shelter and safety.

YOUTH: Our job with you has been to stretch your patience, your boundaries, and your willingness to accept our inevitable growth into now.

PARENTS & YOUTH: It's been an incredible journey—our jobs are changing, we acknowledge this and we will grow to accept that:

PARENTS: Our role with you will become more passive but no less loving.

YOUTH: Our role with you will be to live out what you have sown, growing into new beings through our own experiences.

PARENTS & YOUTH TO CONGREGATION: We ask your help in realizing our recommitment to each other and to you.

DAVID MAYWHOOR

105

From the place where we are right flowers will never grow in the spring.

The place where we are right
is hard and trampled
like a yard.

But doubts and loves dig up the world like a mole, a plow.

And a whisper will be heard in the place
where the ruined
house once stood.

YEHUDA AMICHAI, TRANSLATED BY STEPHEN MITCHELL, ADAPTED

106

Wandering in the dusk,
Sometimes
You get lost in the dusk—

And sometimes not.

Beating your fists
Against the wall,
You break your bones
Against the wall—

But sometimes not.

Walls have been known
To fall,

Dusk turn to dawn,
And chains be gone!

LANGSTON HUGHES, ADAPTED

107

As we weather winds of change,
may we have wisdom to cherish
moments of stillness.

As we recollect times
of challenge and of pain,
may we remember also
the graceful blessings of our lives.

As we look to future unknowns,
may we have the boldness
To trust that there is unimagined
Good
yet to come.

MAUREEN KILLORAN

108

Do more than simply keep the
promises made in your vow.
Do something more: keep promising.
As time passes, keep promising new
things,
deeper things, vaster things, yet
unimagined things.
Promises that will be needed to fill
the expanses of time and of love.
Keep promising.

DAVID BLANCHARD

109

May we go forward in purposeful
rhythm,
that we may give voice to the
melody of our imaginations,
the music of our souls,
and all the possibilities of a just
world
as we might together create it.

Go in Peace.

MATT MEYER

Honoring Ourselves and Others

110

Don't leave your broken heart at the
   door;

Bring it to the altar of life.

Don't leave your anger behind;

*it has high standards
and the world needs vision.*

Bring them with you,

*and your joy
and your passion.*

Bring your loving,

*and your courage
and your conviction.*

Bring your need for healing,

and your powers to heal.

There is work to do

*and you have all that you need to do it
right here in this room.*

Angela Herrera, adapted

111

May this flame we light remind us
   that
every one of us can bring the light of
   love to the world.

May this clear flame be a symbol
that every heart can burn bright with
   joy, peace, and harmony.

May the wisdom of ages speak to us
   through this flame and stay in us.
Every one of us can be a blessing to
   the world.

Petr Samojsky

112

Our church exists to proclaim the
   gospel
that each human being is infinitely
   precious,
that the meaning of our lives lies
   hidden in our interactions with
   each other.

We wish to be a church
where we encounter each other
   with wonder, appreciation, and
   expectation,
where we call out of each other
   strengths, wisdom, and
   compassion
that we never knew we had.

Beverly and David Bumbaugh

113

Each of us, of course, must assume
the responsibility for awakening.

Others may be responsible for our
*   being born,*
but what we make of our lives,
how deeply and intensively we live,
is our responsibility, and ours alone.

Having accepted life as a gift for
    ourselves,
we are then charged to revere the
    presence
of this same gift in others.

FORREST CHURCH, ADAPTED

114

I am a stranger
learning to worship the strangers
around me

whoever you are
whoever I may become.

JUNE JORDAN

115

i am old and need
to remember
you are young and need
to learn
if i forget the words
will you remember the music

NIKKI GIOVANNI

116

Let us simply speak
to one another,
listen and prize the inflections,
never assuming how any person will
    sound
until his mouth opens, until her
mouth opens, greetings welcome
in any language.

ALLISON JOSEPH

117

The bud
stands for all things,
even for those things that don't flower,
for everything flowers, from within,
    of self-blessing;
though sometimes it is necessary
to reteach a thing its loveliness. . . .

GALWAY KINNELL

118

These words are dedicated to those
    who died

because they had no love and felt alone
*   in the world*
because they were afraid to be alone
*   and tried to stick it out*
because they could not ask
because they were shunned
because they were sick and their bodies
*   could not resist the disease*

because they played it safe
because they had no connections
because they had no faith
because they felt they did not belong
and wanted to die

These words are dedicated to those
who died

because they were loners and liked it
because they acquired friends and drew
others to them
because they took risks
because they were stubborn and refused
to give up
because they asked for too much

These words are dedicated to those
who died

because a card was lost and a number
was skipped
because a bed was denied
because a place was filled and no other
place was left

These words are dedicated to those
who died

because someone did not follow
through
because someone was overworked
and forgot
because someone left everything to God
because someone was late
because someone did not arrive at all
because someone told them to wait and
they just couldn't any longer

These words are dedicated to those
who died

because death is a punishment
because death is a reward
because death is the final rest
because death is eternal rage

These words are dedicated to those
who died

Bashert

IRENA KLEPFISZ, ADAPTED

Bashert (Yiddish): inevitable,
(pre)destined

119

These words are dedicated to those
who survived

because their second grade teacher gave
them books
because they did not draw attention to
themselves and got lost in the shuffle
because they knew someone who knew
someone else who could help them
and
bumped into them on a corner on a
Thursday afternoon
because they played it safe
because they were lucky

These words are dedicated to those
who survived

because they knew how to cut corners
because they drew attention to
themselves and always got picked
because they took risks
because they had no principles and
were hard

These words are dedicated to those
who survived

*because they refused to give up and
defied statistics*
*because they had faith and trusted in
God*
*because they expected the worst and
were always prepared*
because they were angry
because they could ask
*because they mooched off others and
saved their strength*
because they endured humiliation
because they turned the other cheek
because they looked the other way

These words are dedicated to those
who survived

*because life is a wilderness and they
were savage*
*because life is an awakening and they
were alert*
*because life is a flowering and they
blossomed*
*because life is a struggle and they
struggled*
*because life is a gift and they were free
to accept it*

These words are dedicated to those
who survived

Bashert

IRENA KLEPFISZ, ADAPTED

*Bashert (Yiddish): inevitable,
(pre)destined*

120

READER 1: I don't have anything to say.

READER 2: Well, I do—but it might
not be interesting to anyone.

READER 1: I have secrets inside of me,
and struggles, and I don't know
if I'm ready to share them.

READER 2: I want to hear what you
have to say.

READER 1: I want to speak of the
deepest things together.

READER 2: I want to hear what you
dream about, what you hope for.

READER 1: I want to know how you
have come to arrive at this resting
point along your journey.

READER 2: What if I speak and you
don't understand me?

READER 1: I will listen, and listen
again, until my hearing becomes
understanding.

READER 2: What if can't find the
words to share the world inside
of me?

READER 1: I believe that wise words
will emerge from you.

READER 2: How can I trust you to
hold my life's stories? You, who
I may not even know?

READER 1: By knowing that, as I
receive part of your story, I will
give you part of mine.

READER 2: How will this work? What will happen? What awaits us?

READER 1: We can find out anything by beginning.

READER 2: Let us begin to listen, and trust, and to know one another more deeply.

ERIKA HEWITT

121

We meet in the spaces between us:

stillness;
music,
heard or unheard,

the apparent void teeming
with the you and the I that overlap,
in this one sacred living moment.

We meet in the spaces between us.

AMY CAROL WEBB

122

When strangers meet, endless
possibilities emerge:

New experiences, new ways of
understanding, and new ways of
taking action.

When strangers meet, each pays
special attention to the other.

Each is called to serve something larger
than the self.
Today, this morning, let's light the chalice:
for openness,

for willingness to grow,

for rich curiosity,

and for common purpose.

FULGENCE NDAGIJAMANA

123

All people are children when they
sleep.

There's no war in them then.
They open their hands and breathe
in that quiet rhythm heaven has given
them.

They pucker their lips like small
children
and open their hands halfway,
soldiers and statesmen, servants and
masters.

The stars stand guard
and a haze veils the sky,
a few hours when no one will do
anybody harm.

If only we could speak to one
another then
when our hearts are half-open
flowers.

Words like golden bees
would drift in.

—God, teach me the language of
sleep.

ROLF JACOBSEN, TRANSLATED BY
ROBERT HEDIN, ADAPTED

124

The time will come
When, with elation,
You will greet yourself arriving
At your own door, in your own mirror,
and each will smile at the other's
    welcome,

And say, sit here. Eat.
You will love again the stranger who
    was your self.
Give wine. Give bread. Give back your
    heart
To itself, to the stranger who has loved
    you

All your life, whom you ignored
For another, who knows you by heart.
Take down the love letters from the
    bookshelf,

The photographs, the desperate notes,
Peel your own image from the mirror.
Sit. Feast on your life.

DEREK WALCOTT, ADAPTED

Interconnectedness

125

May the light of this chalice give light
   and warmth to our community,
when we are joyful and when we
   despair.
And may we feel the warmth spread
   from our circle
to wider and wider circles,
until all know they belong
to the one circle of life.

BETSY DARR, ADAPTED

126

Glory be to the earth and the wind.
Glory be to the sun and the rain.
Glory be to animals and children. . . .
Glory be to our holy flame,
   which calls us together as one.

BETTYE A. DOTY

127

The stuff I need for singing by
   whatever means
is garnered from every thought, every
   heart that ever pounded the
   earth. . . .
The shapes of mountains, cities, a
   whistle leaf of grass, or a human
   bent with loss
will revise the pattern of the story,
   the song.

I take it from there, . . . play through
   the heartbreak of the tenderness of
   being
until I am the sky, the earth, the song
   and the singer.

JOY HARJO

128

We affirm that every one of us is held
   in Creation's hand—
a part of the interdependent cosmic
   web—
and hence strangers need not be
   enemies;
that no one is saved until we All are
   saved
where All means the whole of Creation.

WILLIAM SCHULZ

129

They asked, "If a tree should fall in
   the woods and you are not there,
   does it make a sound?"

And the answer came, "If a tree should
   fall and no one is there, listen for
   the cry of mourning birds who
   grieve the loss of their nests. They
   know where the tree lies. They call
   you to companion them as they
   search for a place to rest. Listen
   then, for the mourning birds."

AARON R. PAYSON

130

Come and find me.
You won't have to look hard.
Come to where the ocean touches the
  shore;
find me in the bright-light promise
  of morning on the waves;
look carefully at the bubbles breaking
  on the wet sand—there I am.
Turn over the glistening rock, slippery
  with its cushion of seaweed—here
  I am.
Hear the gulls crying news of the
  endless ocean—that is my news,
  my voice.
Lie with me in the tall, green marsh
  grass;
see my footprints in the sand you
  have walked upon.
Do not say I am lost, for you have
  found me. I am here.

ELIZABETH TARBOX, ADAPTED

131

But it is hard to speak of these things:

*how the voices of light enter the body
and begin to recite their stories*

how the earth holds us painfully
  against
its breast made of humus and
  brambles

*how we who will soon be gone regard
the entities that continue to return
greener than ever,*

spring water flowing
through a meadow and the shadows
  of clouds
passing over the hills

*and the ground
where we stand in the tremble of
  thought
taking the vast outside into ourselves.*

BILLY COLLINS, ADAPTED

132

Children widen the circle of our
  being in ways that are limitless.

*Every baby that's born connects us to
our history, our own mothers and
fathers, grandparents and unknown
forbears who brought new life to the
world in each successive generation.*

Every baby that's born links us to
  the future, to a world yet to come
  that belongs to our descendants
  and that we hold in trust for our
  posterity whom we will never
  know.

*Each child that's born connects us
to nature, to the innocence and
exuberance of a world always
hatching newborns: kittens and
pups and lambs and babes.*

Each child reminds us of the kinship
   we share with people of other lands
   and races who love their young as
   purely and tenderly as we do.

Each child connects us to the universe,
   to the holy mysteries of birth and
   death and becoming from which we
   all emerge.

Children widen the circle of our
   being in ways that are limitless.

GARY KOWALSKI

Our respect for other people, for
   other nations, and for other
   cultures
can only grow from a humble respect
   for the cosmic order

and from an awareness that we are a
   part of it, that we share in it,
and that nothing of what we do is lost,
   but rather becomes part
of the eternal memory of Being, where
   it is judged.

VÁCLAV HAVEL, ADAPTED

133

We are one, after all, you and I;

together we suffer,
together exist,

and forever will recreate each other.

PIERRE TEILHARD DE CHARDIN,
ADAPTED

134

We must divest ourselves of our
   egoistical anthropocentrism,
our habit of seeing ourselves as
   masters of the universe
who can do whatever occurs to us.

We must discover a new respect for
   what transcends us:
for the universe, for the earth, for
   nature, for life, and for reality.

135

We are all things, all persons,

full and famished, good and
   bewildered,
sly and honest, frightened and less
   frightened, killer and slain,
the rapturer and the enraptured,
youth and age, male and female,
baby and corpse.

We are all things,

tree and flower, moss and grass,
   mammal and reptile, bird and insect.

The creature that is life is apart from
   nothing that lives.

KENNETH PATTON, ADAPTED

136

I swear there is no greatness or power
 that does not
emulate those of the earth,

*There can be no theory of any account
 unless it
corroborate the theory of the earth,*

No politics, song, religion, behavior,
 or what not,
is of account, unless it compare
 with the
amplitude of the earth,

*Unless it face the exactness, vitality,
 impartiality,
Rectitude of the earth.*

    WALT WHITMAN, ADAPTED

137

Out of a community of diverse
 heritage and belief,

*we come together to share our hope,
 and to create good in the world.*

The prophets of all traditions and
 times have taught
that we are called to mercy,
 generosity, and mutual care,

and that to be great is to serve.

We know that there can be no
 enduring happiness for humanity
so long as suffering and want go
 unrelieved;

*until all may be sheltered, none of us is
truly at home.*

May the power of our various faiths
 sustain us in this work,
that we may be the hands of holy
 creativity and justice;

and together build a better world.

    KENDYL GIBBONS

138

As we gather to celebrate
the season of birth and rebirth,

We hear the heart beat of Mother Earth

With spring comes the blossoming
 of plants
and emerging patterns of life

We hear the heart beat of Mother Earth

In this the time of growth and
 reflection
let us draw closer to nature and each
 other

We hear the heart beat of Mother Earth

ALL: In the continuing circle of life,
 giving thanks,
 we hear the heart beat of Mother
 Earth

    ADDAE AMA KRABA

139

It's an earth song—
And I've been waiting long
For an earth song.

It's a spring song!
I've been waiting long
For a spring song:

Strong as the bursting of young buds,
Strong as the shoots of a new plant,
Strong as the coming of the first child
From its mother's womb—

An earth song!

A body song!

A spring song!

And I've been waiting long
For an earth song.

LANGSTON HUGHES, ADAPTED

140

The mountains,

I become part of it . . .

The herbs, the fir tree,

I become part of it.

The morning mists, the clouds, the
    gathering waters,

I become part of it.

The wilderness, the dew drops, the
    pollen . . .

I become part of it.

NAVAJO CHANT

141

Remember the earth whose skin you
    are:
red earth, black earth, yellow earth,
    white earth
brown earth.

We are earth.

Remember the plants, trees, animal
    life who all have their
tribes, their families, their histories,
    too. Talk to them,
listen to them. They are alive poems.
Remember the wind. Remember her
    voice. She knows the
origin of this universe.
Remember you are all people and all
    people are you.

We are earth.

Remember you are this universe and
    this
universe is you.

We are earth.

Remember all is in motion, is
    growing, is you.

We are earth.

Remember language comes from
    this.
Remember the dance language is,
    that life is.
Remember.

We are earth.

JOY HARJO, ADAPTED

142

Let us be united;
Let us speak in harmony;
Let our minds apprehend alike.
Common be our prayer;
Common be the end of our assembly;
Common be our resolution;
Common be our deliberations.
Alike be our feelings;
Unified be our hearts;
Common be our intentions;
Perfect be our unity.

RIG VEDA

143

Spirit that hears each one of us,
Hears all that is—
Listens, listens, hears us out—
Inspire us now!
Our own pulse beats in every
stranger's throat,
And also there within the flowered
ground beneath
     our feet,
And—teach us to listen!—
We can hear it in water, in wood,
and even in stone.
We are earth of this earth, and we
are bone of its bone.
This is a prayer I sing, for we have
forgotten this
     and so
The earth is perishing.

BARBARA DEMING

Justice

144

The truth is this:
if here is no justice,
there will be no peace.

*If we cannot bring justice into the
small circles of our individual lives,
we cannot hope to bring justice to the
world.*

And if we do not bring justice to the
world,
none of us is safe and none of us will
survive.

*Nothing that we do is more important
than making justice real—
here, where we are.*

ALL: Hard as diversity is, it is our
most important task.

ROSEMARY BRAY MCNATT

145

A principle is a principle,
and in no case can it be watered
down
because of our incapacity to live it
in practice. We have to strive to
achieve it,
and the striving should be conscious,
deliberate and hard.

MAHATMA GANDHI

146

It is not enough merely to call for
freedom, democracy and human
rights.

*There has to be a united determination
to persevere in the struggle,
to make sacrifices in the name of
enduring truths,
to resist the corrupting influences of
desire, ill will, ignorance and fear.*

AUNG SAN SUU KYI, ADAPTED

147

Again this procession of the speechless
Bringing me their words
The future woke me with its silence
I join the procession
An open doorway
Speaks for me
Again

W.S. MERWIN

148

That dream
shall have a name
after all,
and it will not be vengeful
but wealthy with love
and compassion

and knowledge.
And it will rise
in this heart
which is our America.

SIMON ORTIZ

149

This is where we are.

Where do we go from here?

First, we must massively assert our
dignity and worth.

*We must stand up amidst a system
that still oppresses
and develop an unassailable and
majestic sense of values. . . .*

What is needed is a realization that
power without love
is reckless and abusive,

*and that love without power is
sentimental and anemic.*

Power at its best is love implementing
the demands of justice,

*and justice at its best is power correcting
everything that stands against love.*

And this is what we must see as we
move on.

MARTIN LUTHER KING JR.,
ADAPTED

150

Religion and Justice are borne on
each other's wings. What makes
them such soulmates?

*Every single one of us knows what it
is like to bleed. Every one of us has
experienced pain.*

If that were not a fact of human
existence, we might not notice
the suffering of the world.

Because it is, we do.

Every single one of us knows what
it is like to bleed. In one respect
pain is a gift because it cultivates
our imagination. Without it, we
would be far less likely to rail at
deprivation or shrink from cruelty.

*In the heart of every stranger lurks a
reflection of our own.*

WILLIAM SCHULZ, ADAPTED

151

We understand it still that there is no
easy road to freedom.

*We know it well that none of us acting
alone can achieve success.*

We must therefore act together as a
united people, for national
reconciliation, for nation building,
for the birth of a new world.

Let there be justice for all.

Let there be peace for all.

*Let there be work, bread, water and
salt for all.*

Let each know that for each the body,
the mind and the soul have been
freed to fulfill themselves.

Let freedom reign.

NELSON MANDELA, ADAPTED

152

History, despite its wrenching pain
Cannot be unlived, but if faced
With courage, need not be lived again.

Lift up your eyes upon
The day breaking for you.
Give birth again
To the dream.

MAYA ANGELOU

153

And I dream of our coming together

*encircled   driven
not only by love*

but by lust for a working tomorrow

*the flights of this journey
mapless   uncertain*

and necessary as water.

AUDRE LORDE, ADAPTED

154

We who dwell on the margins
know about divisions, arbitrary and
    intentional,
like land,
like class,
like culture

*We make sharp borders around pieces
    of our selves,
and we blur the edges
by being who we are,
by expanding the circle.*

Beyond binaries, we multiply
    possibilities—
languages, customs, practices,
rituals, and ceremonies—
not one narrative but stories shared.

*Separation is illusion.
Love transgresses borders
between you, me, us, them,
between secular and sacred.*

We need trust to strengthen our
    connection.
We must dare to cross
from my world into yours, from
    your world into mine,
until we begin to weave a tapestry
    of faith,
and wonder aloud:

*Whose are we?
What is a nation?
Who can own the Earth?*

WENDY BARTEL

155

Why are the nations in an uproar?
Why do the peoples mutter and
  threaten?
Why do the rich plot with the
  powerful?

*They are rebelling against the demands
  of Love and Justice.*

God laughs, cries, and says with
  anger:

*I have set my Love in your hearts and
  my Justice in your minds.*
*You are my children and I have given
  you the universe,*
your lives, and the tasks of your days.

Be wise.

Be warned.

Stick to the paths of Love and Justice.
Your restless hearts will find me there.

CHRISTINE ROBINSON,
INSPIRED BY PSALM 2

156

Part of the ugliness of my heart is the
  ugliness of the clear cut forest.
Part of the fear in my heart is the
  fear in the heart of the ghetto
as well as in the heart of the gated
  community.
Part of the anger in my heart is the
  anger in the heart of the abused
  child.

The ignorance and sloth and greed in
  the world is reflected in my heart.
And how shall I heal?
How shall I overcome these things
  in my heart
if I do not work to overcome them
  in the world?
How shall I approach the divine if
  I turn from its appearance in the
  world,
even in the person of the least of
  these, my relatives all around me?

KEN COLLIER

157

What is essential is never to allow
The limitations of time and the
Erosion of memories to deaden
The longing of the heart in
Its morning demand for love.

PAUL N. CARNES

158

The question is not whether we will
  be extremists,

but what kind of extremists will we be.

Will we be extremists for hate or for
  love?

*Will we be extremists for the
  preservation of injustice
or for the extension of justice?*

MARTIN LUTHER KING, JR.

159

We are a gentle and generous people.
But let us not forget our anger.

May it fuel not only our commitment to
compassion but also our commitment
to make fundamental changes.

Our vision of the Beloved Community
must stand against a vision that
would allow the privilege of the few
to be accepted as just and even holy.

Our religious vision must again and
again ask "Who is my neighbor?"
and strive always to include more
and more of us.

As we intone the words that gave birth
to this nation, "We the people. . . ."
We are, and we should be, both a
gentle, and an angry people.

WILLIAM SINKFORD, ADAPTED

Living Tradition

160

A chalice lit in our midst is a symbol
of our liberal faith:
A faith built on the foundations of
freedom, reason, and welcome
A faith sustained by acts of kindness
and justice
A faith that envisions a world
flourishing, with equality for all
people
A faith that demands the living out
of goodness
A faith that requires thoughtfulness
A faith of wholeness

This tiny flame is the symbol of the
spark of all this within each of us.

DEBRA FAULK

161

We come together today
to honor the universal community of
seekers to which we all belong.

We gather together today to share from
our deepest place of safety
that we might nurture ourselves by
celebrating one another.

We call into our presence this hour
our ancestors
whose love, labor, and commitment
made it possible for us to be here now.

Let us call one another to the table of
abundance
that we may feed on those fruits
that sustain us and ever ask us to
grow.

Let us open to this moment
with hearts that have no borders.

MARTA I. VALENTÍN

162

Hoy nos reunimos
para honrar a la communidad
universal
en constante busqueda
a la cual pertenecemos todos.

Nos reunimos hoy para compartir
desde una seguridad profunda
que nosotros nos sostenemos en la
celebración de cada uno.

Invocamos la presencia de nuestros
ancestros, su amor, su trabajo y
sus compromisos,
que hicieron posible que estemos aquí
ahora.

Invitemos a la mesa de la abundancia
a cada uno de nosotros
para comer de estos frutos
que nos sostienen y nos piden que
sigamos creciendo.

Que en este momento
se abran nuestros corazones sin
    fronteras.

> MARTA I. VALENTÍN,
> TRANSLATED BY MARIA
> CRISTINA VLASSIDIS BURGOA
> AND IRÉNE DURAND BRYAN

163

Unitarian Universalists have said for centuries that there is room in our religion for all seekers. Skeptics and poets and scientists are welcome here, as are nonconformists and shy and uncertain folk. We believe that restlessness and doubts are a sign of grace, that the love of truth is the holiest of gifts.

> BARBARA MERRITT

164

We are here dedicated to the
    proposition that,
beneath all our differences,
behind all our diversity,
there is a unity that binds us forever
    together,
in spite of time and death and the
    space between the stars.
We pause in silent witness to that
    unity.

> DAVID BUMBAUGH

165

Our religion is a religion of social
    concern,
a religion of intellectual and ethical
    integrity,
a religion that emphasizes the
    dynamic conception of history
and the scientific worldview,
a religion that stresses the dignity and
    worth of the person as a supreme
    value
and goodwill as the creative force in
    human relations.
This religion can and ought to
    become a beacon from which this
    kind of faith shines.

> LEWIS A. MCGEE

166

A living tradition is not bequeathed
through some law of inheritance;
it must be earned, not without dust
    and heat,
and not without humbling grace.

> JAMES LUTHER ADAMS

167

Unitarian Universalism is
faith in people, hope for tomorrow's
    child,
confidence in a continuity that spans
    all time.

*It looks not to a perfect heaven, but
    toward a good earth.*

It is respectful of the past, but not
limited to it.

*It is trust in growing and conspiracy
with change.*

It is spiritual responsibility for a
moral tomorrow.

EDWARD L. SCHEMPP

168

We are Unitarian Universalists.
With minds that think,
Hearts that love,
And hands that are ready to serve.
Together we care for our Earth,
And work for friendship and peace in
our world.

AISHA HAUSER AND
SUSAN LAWRENCE

169

We, the members of this congregation
express to this congregation's Board
of Trustees
our gratitude for your investment
in our community,
our trust in your integrity and
wisdom,
our support of your leadership,
and our enduring loyalty to the
mission and vision of this church.

We pledge to do what is within our
power
to make your stewardship of our
shared future

an experience of discovery,
accomplishment, and growth.

Together may we make this
community a beacon of reason,
compassion, and freedom,
and a witness to the power of love
and aspiration to make a better
world.

KENDYL GIBBONS

170

I am a part of history.
I am connected to a family and
forebears.
I am part of humanity
I am heir to all that humans have
brought to the world.
I am part of nature.
I am what the stars are.

MARK BELLETINI,
INSPIRED BY DAVID RICHO

171

Ah, it's true.

*When our ancestors spoke of heaven,
they were speaking of this moment.*

When they went on about nirvana
they imagined a time like this.

*When they sang of paradise,
it was this morning they imagined.*

A time when all the mysteries of life
and death
are blended in a community of praise,

when the bones of ancient lovers
are given flesh again in our own
    bodies,
teachers of long ago speaking of love
    and truth
once more in lives so ordinary they are
extraordinary.

Blest is our breath, in and out, quiet,

blest is our sitting, our fidgeting, our
    movement,

*blest is our heartbeat echoing the
    pounding alleluias of the distant
    stars,*

blest is the silence that is presence,

not absence.

MARK BELLETINI, ADAPTED

172

Always there is a beginning—

a new day,
a new month,
a new season,
a new year.

Forever the old passes away

and newness emerges
from the richness that was.

Nothing is ever lost

in the many changes
time brings.

What was, in some way,
will be,

though changed in form.

Always there is a beginning—

a new day,
a new month,
a new season,
a new year.

EDWARD SEARL, ADAPTED

173

The growing good of the world
is partly dependent on unhistoric acts;
and that things are not so ill
with you and me
as they might have been,
is half owing to the number
who lived faithfully a hidden life,
and rest in unvisited tombs.

GEORGE ELIOT

174

Stories are for joining the past to the
    future.

*Stories are for those late hours in the
    night*
when you can't remember how you got
from where you were to where you are.

Stories are for eternity, when memory
    is erased,
when there is nothing to remember
    except the story.

TIM O'BRIEN, ADAPTED

175

To acknowledge our ancestors means
we are aware that we did not make
ourselves,
that the line stretches
all the way back, perhaps, to God; or
to Gods. We remember them
 because it
is an easy thing to forget: that we
are not the first to suffer, rebel,
fight, love and die. The grace with
which we embrace life, in spite of
the pain, the sorrows, is always a
measure of what has gone before.

ALICE WALKER

176

Can you hear them?
Can you hear the whispers of the
 ancestors?

We remember.
Their stories are in these walls, in our
 bones, in the air that we breathe.
Their stories are in the touch of a
 calloused hand,
in the melody of songs that we hum
 while washing dishes,
in remembered faces.

We hear the whispers of the ancestors
how their stories touch our lives
and call us into becoming.

LYNN GARDNER

177

LEADER: The living tradition which
 we share draws from many
 sources:

LEFT: Direct experience of that
 transcending mystery and
 wonder, affirmed in all cultures,
 which moves us to a renewal
 of the spirit and an openness
 to the forces which create and
 uphold life;

RIGHT: Words and deeds of prophetic
 women and men which challenge
 us to confront powers and
 structures of evil with justice,
 compassion, and the
 transforming power of love;

LEFT: Wisdom from the world's
 religions which inspires us in
 our ethical and spiritual life;

RIGHT: Jewish and Christian teachings
 which call us to respond to
 God's love by loving our
 neighbors as ourselves;

LEFT: Humanist teachings which
 counsel us to heed the guidance
 of reason and the results of
 science, and warn us against
 idolatries of the mind and spirit;

RIGHT: Spiritual teachings of earth-
 centered traditions which
 celebrate the sacred circle of
 life and instruct us to live in
 harmony with the rhythms of
 nature.

ALL: Grateful for the religious pluralism which enriches and ennobles our faith, we are inspired to deepen our understanding and expand our vision. As free congregations we enter into this covenant, promising to one another our mutual trust and support.

ADAPTED BY ROGER JONES

178

Who are these children, that we are mindful of them?

They are our present delight.
By them we are reminded of life's small joys and wisdoms.

They are the heirs of the work that we have done and are doing,
the next generation unto whom the torch of our tradition shall pass from our hands.

They shall build upon the foundations that we lay.

They are the yet unwritten chapter in the story of our faith.

This being the case, what do we promise unto them, and to their parents?

We pledge them our love and support,
a listening ear and a helping hand in times of trial.

We pledge them a community of openmindedness,
a place where their beliefs, their doubts, and their questions are received with gentleness and respect.

We pledge them challenge,
skepticism of the too-easy answer, and a pointing to the ever-open road.

We pledge them roots; a tradition to pass on to their own children,
a place to come home to.

KENDYL GIBBONS

179

We are here

as we are—

mortal, concerned, life-affirming,

turned toward joy, facing our woes—

to worship, to behold the mysteries of life and death
without shield of creed

May our celebration,
help move us into that company
who lived to unveil ever-deeper truth,
who yielded their faithfulness
when history's hard press was upon them,
who honed their lives,
no less fragile or strong than our own,
on the whetstone of your demands and ecstasies, O love.

Life of our own lives, we begin again

MARK BELLETINI, ADAPTED

180

We bring into our hearts all those
who have gone before us:
all those whose living in this world
has prepared the soil for our living,
all those whose being has enabled our
being.

*Let us also remember those whose
existence is seeded in our lives today,
not only those who are our physical
descendants
but also those whose spirits inherit the
love we sow,
the hope we reap, the promise we harvest.*

And may those of us whose religious
inheritance is freedom
never rest until all who wish to be its
children are sheltered.

LESLIE TAKAHASHI

181

This is what we do with our faith:

*Live in this world knowing that we
will lose each other,*

loving despite the hard bargain it
demands of us,

*doing what we can so that truth may
be safely lived,*

measuring our faith by the difference
we have made,

*building up faith communities to
continue after we are gone.*

JUDITH MEYER

182

Let us recognize that, as parents,
we do not raise our children by
ourselves.

*Let us remember, as children, how
many people it takes
to bring our being into existence.*

Let us praise those who have created
us and
bequeathed to us the gifts of life:

*Let us praise our mother and our father
for our genetic legacy
and for the care they have given us.*

Let us also praise those who have
preserved
and passed on our great cultural
heritage.

*Let us praise those who have nourished
us physically,
but also those who have stimulated our
minds and fed our spirits;*

those who have created a home for us,
but those also who labor so long to
make the world more homelike.

*As we praise these people,
let us vow to hand down this legacy,
not merely to our own children,
but to all the children of the earth.*

BARBARA ROHDE, ADAPTED

183

There is only one reason for joining a Unitarian Universalist church and that is to support it.

We want to support it because

it stands against superstition and fear.

We want to support it because

this church points to what is noblest and best in human life.

We want to support it because

it is open to women and men of whatever religion, race, creed, color, place of origin, political affiliation, gender identity, or sexual orientation.

We want to support it because

it is a place where children can learn that religion is for joy, comfort, gratitude, and love.

We want to support it because

it is a place where walls between people are torn down rather than built-up.

We want to support it because

it is more concerned with human beings than with dogmas.

We want to support it because

it searches for the holy, rather than dwelling upon the depraved.

We want to support it because

it calls no one a sinner, yet knows how deep is the struggle in each person's breast and how great is the hunger for what is good.

We want to support it because

it calls us to worship what is truly worthy of our sacrifice.

There is only one reason for joining a Unitarian Universalist church:

to support it.

JOHN B. WOLF, ADAPTED

Love

184

Even when our hearts are broken
by our own failure
or the failure of others
cutting into our lives,
even when we have done all we can
and life is still broken,
there is a Universal Love
that has never broken faith with us
and never will.

REBECCA ANN PARKER

185

We are weaned from our timidity

*In the flush of love's light
we dare be brave*

And suddenly we see
that love costs all we are
and will ever be.

*Yet it is only love
Which sets us free.*

MAYA ANGELOU, ADAPTED

186

For nothing is fixed,

forever, forever, forever,

it is not fixed;

the earth is always shifting,

the light is always changing,

the sea does not cease to grind down rock.

Generations do not cease to be born,
and we are responsible to them
because we are the only witnesses they
have.

*The sea rises, the light fails,
lovers cling to each other,
and children cling to us.*

The moment we cease to hold each
other,

*the moment we break faith with one
another,*

the sea engulfs us and the light goes
out.

JAMES BALDWIN, ADAPTED

187

Love is the only magic—

It enriches the giver

as it nourishes the object.

It serves the instant

and washes over the ages.

It is as particular as the moon

and as universal as the heavens.

If returned it is multiplied,

yet spurned it is not diminished.

PATRICK MURFIN

188

Oh, the comfort—

the inexpressible comfort

of feeling safe with a person—

having neither to weigh thoughts

nor measure words,

but pouring them all right out,

just as they are,

chaff and grain together;

certain that a faithful hand will take
   and sift them,
keep what is worth keeping,

and then with the breath of kindness

blow the rest away.

DINAH MARIA MULOCK CRAIK,
ADAPTED

189

Has my heart gone to sleep?
Have the beehives of my dreams
stopped working, the waterwheel
of the mind run dry,
scoops turning empty,
only shadow inside?

No, my heart is not asleep.
It is awake, wide awake.
Not asleep, not dreaming—
its eyes are opened wide
watching distant signals, listening
on the rim of the vast silence.

ANTONIO MACHADO, TRANSLATED
BY ALAN S. TRUEBLOOD

190

¿Mi corazón se ha dormido?
Colmenares de mis sueños
¿ya no labráis? ¿Está seca
la noria del pensamiento,
los cangilones vacíos,
girando, de sombra llenos?

No, mi corazón no duerme.
Está despierto, despierto.
Ni duerme ni sueña, mira,
los claros ojos abiertos,
señas lejanas y escucha
a orillas del gran silencio.

ANTONIO MACHADO

191

The time has come we must defend
   our dream,
proclaim *this* as what is best in us.
Where would we be without our
   variant love?
The world would shrivel, die.
   Without surprise
boredom would be the sole master
   of space
and summer joys would perish under
   constant snow.

STEVE ABBOTT

192

When the great plates slip,
and the earth shivers,
and the flaw is seen to lie in what you
    trusted most,

look not to more solidity,
to weighty slabs of concrete poured
or strength of cantilevered beam
to save the fractured order.

Trust more the tensile strands of love
that bend and stretch
to hold you in the web of life
that's often torn but always healing.

The shifting plates, the restive earth,
your room, your precious life,
they all proceed from love,
the ground on which we walk together.

    ROBERT R. WALSH, ADAPTED

193

Love is knotted and gnarled,
like an old tree fighting with the wind,
like branches too brittle for their own
    good,
like roots that relentlessly inform
how deeply we can trust and how
    freely we can forgive.

    JAN CARLSSON-BULL

194

Love is anterior to life,
    Posterior to death,
Initial of creation, and
    The exponent of breath.

    EMILY DICKINSON

195

Life is too brief
Between the budding and the falling
    leaf,
Between the seed time and the golden
    sheaf,
For hate and spite.
We have no time for malice and for
    greed:
Therefore, with love make beautiful
    the deed;
Fast speeds the night.

    W.M. VORIES

196

Choose to bless the world!

The choice to bless the world is more
    than an act of will
    a moving forward into the world
with the intention to do good.
It is an act of recognition,
    a confession of surprise,
    a grateful acknowledgment
that in the midst of a broken world
unspeakable beauty, grace and
    mystery abide. . . .

None of us alone can save the world. Together—that is another possibility, waiting.

REBECCA ANN PARKER, ADAPTED

197

When death comes suddenly, taking
    just one friend,
or in a magnitude beyond our
    comprehension,

in horror and disbelief, we remember.

When bright and innocent lives are
    cut short,
without warning or mercy,

in agony and outrage, we remember.

When a long life closes with honor
    and thankfulness,

*in reluctant submission and gratitude,
    we remember.*

When bereavement and loss seem to
    be everywhere we turn,
and the world goes dark,

in emptiness and pain, we remember.

When help and comfort must be
    given to the afflicted,
and the work of our hands is needed,

in duty and sacrifice, we remember.

When arrangements must be made,
and the severed threads bound up,

in ritual and custom, we remember.

When it feels that nothing matters,
and life as it once was seems distant
    and unreal,

in sorrow and numbness, we remember.

When grief comes upon us in waves,
and the helpless heart overflows,

*in sadness and aching tears, we
    remember.*

When words at last become
    meaningless,
and the only peace lies inward,

in silence and solitude, we remember.

When communities come together,
    and the hurt is shared,
*in mutual comfort and consolation,
    we remember.*

When a strain of music, or a familiar
    image,
brings a gentle, wistful smile,

*in tenderness and nostalgia, we
    remember.*

When the spirit of life beckons us
    to lift our eyes
to all that remains true and good,

in dedication and trust, we remember.

When the lessons of mutual help
    and understanding taught by
    tragedy live on in us to bless the
    world,

in love and kinship, we remember.

When we come to honor those we
have lost
by learning to cherish more dearly
those around us,

*in generosity and gratitude, we
remember.*

KENDYL GIBBONS

198

We are.

Therefore we love. . . .

We love.

Therefore, we are.

May we be humble before the wonder
Of what we dare to create.

RICHARD S. GILBERT, ADAPTED

199

READER 1: If you come as softly
As wind within the trees
You may hear what I hear
See what sorrow sees.

READER 2: If you come as lightly
As threading dew
I will take you gladly
Nor ask more of you.

READER 1: You may sit beside me
Silent as a breath
Only those who stay dead
Shall remember death.

READER 2: And if you come I will be
silent
Nor speak harsh words to you.
I will not ask you why, now.
Or how, or what you do.

BOTH: We shall sit here, softly
Beneath two different years
And the rich earth between us
Shall drink our tears.

AUDRE LORDE, ADAPTED

200

Love which is the most difficult
mystery
Asking from every young one answers
And most from those most eager and
most beautiful—

Love is a bird in a fist:
To hold it hides it, to look at it lets it go.

It will twist loose if you lift so much
as a finger.
It will stay if you cover it—stay but
unknown and invisible.

Either you keep it forever with fist closed
Or let it fling

Singing in fervor of sun and in song
vanish.
There is no answer other to this
mystery.

ARCHIBALD MACLEISH, ADAPTED

201

Love, if it is love, never goes away.

It is embedded in us,
like seams of gold in the Earth,

waiting for light,

waiting to be struck.

ALICE WALKER, ADAPTED

202

Love, you are strong as a dark blue
mountain.

Love, you are as fluid as a wide silver
river.

Love, you are as splendid as a clear
night sky.

Love, you are as mysterious as a dark
forest.

Love, you are as wise as enduring
friendship.

Love, you are true power, not mere
distraction
truth, not deceit,
purpose, not impulse,
poetry, not prose,
sing not sang,
now more than tomorrow,
but tomorrow more than yesterday.

Love, condense yourself into this
moment,
permeate the silence that joins us in
community,

so that in the fire of the words to
come,
the promises of this hour
might be sealed in peace.

Amen.

MARK BELLETINI

203

Go now in peace.
Deeply regard each other;
Truly listen to each other;
Speak what each must speak;
Be ready in every moment to disarm
your own heart;
Rejoice in this love you have begun.
Amen.

BARBARA HAMILTON-HOLWAY

204

In the end it won't matter how much
we have,

but how generously we have given.

It won't matter how much we know,

but rather how well we live.

And it won't matter how much we
believe,

but how deeply we love.

JOHN MORGAN

205

Let the love of this hour go on; let all
  the oaths and
  children and people of this love be
  clean as a
  washed stone under a waterfall in
  the sun.

CARL SANDBURG

206

The Chalice is extinguished,
but its light lives on in the minds
  and the hearts and the souls of
  each one of us.

Let us carry the flame with us and
  share it with those we know,
with those we love, and most
  especially, with those we have yet
  to meet.

BRIAN KIELY

207

Often we are found in our grief and
  comforted
calmed by some kindness
brought alive again by beauty
that catches us undefended.

*Even when the sun is most thin and far
even at the hour the storm is at its
  height . . .*

*renewal nests within sorrow
love abides, even beyond anger, beyond
  death.*

We are held in an embrace invisible
  but infinite
moving with all creation
between wholeness and fragmentation
moving always toward the one. . . .

Love, do not let us go.   Amen.

BARBARA J. PESCAN, ADAPTED

208

Great voice that calls us in the wind
  of dawn,
Strange voice that stills us in the heat
  of noon,

*Heard in the sunset,
Heard in the moonrise*

And in the stirring of the wakeful
  night,

*Speak now in blessing,
Chide us no longer,*

Great voice of love, we will not grieve
  thee more.

EDNA ST. VINCENT MILLAY,
ADAPTED

209

O God, you surround us.
In you we have our being.
Help us to recognize the love that
     surrounds us.
Help us to see ourselves as the loving
     people we are and can be.
In silence, now, we bring to our
     mind's eye the people who have
loved us and continue to love us,
people who are not here with us
     today, but whose love we carry
     with us;
people who are there every day, and
     whose love we sometimes take for
     granted,
people who might be within our
     circle of love,
could we but extend it a little further.
In silence, now, we hold these people
     in our hearts.

[*silence*]

In returning from silence, we ask that
     our hearts may be opened
to all whose names and faces have
     crossed our minds
and that the love we share with the
     people in our lives may be our
     abiding teacher.

WAYNE B. ARNASON

Peace

210

All will come again into its strength:
the fields undivided, the waters
    undammed,
the trees towering and the walls built
    low.
And in the valleys, people as strong
and varied as the land.

And no churches where God
is imprisoned and lamented
like a trapped and wounded animal.
The houses welcoming all who knock
and a sense of boundless offering
in all relations, and in you and me.

No yearning for an afterlife, no
    looking beyond,
no belittling of death,
but only a longing for what belongs
    to us,
and serving earth, lest we remain
    unused.

RAINER MARIA RILKE, TRANSLATED BY
ANITA BARROWS AND JOANNA MACY

211

Who are these among you
Homesick for home, longing for
    peace—
The summer going and the war going
And all the sharp promises of peace?

Watch from your foxholes
For fire on distant mountains,

Fire flags lit with peace
Waving on the mountains.

There are other journeys
You must make after your journey
    home,

Other journeys you must make alone
Into the countries of the heart
To sit with silence and decide alone.

OWEN DODSON, ADAPTED

212

In the end, of course, a true war story
    is never about war.

It's about sunlight.

It's about the special way that dawn
    spreads out on a river
when you know you must cross the
    river and march into the mountains
and do things you are afraid to do.

It's about love and memory.
It's about sorrow.
It's about people who never listen.

TIM O'BRIEN, ADAPTED

213

And the servants of Allah Most
    Gracious
are those who walk on the earth in
    humility,

and when the ignorant address them,
they say, "Peace!"

QUR'AN 25:63, TRANSLATED BY
ABDULLAH YUSUF ALI, ADAPTED

214

Our first task in approaching another
    people,
another culture,
another religion,
is to take off our shoes,
for the place we are approaching is
    holy.
Else we find ourselves treading on
    others' dreams.

MAX WARREN, ADAPTED

215

This is a house of peace.
Breathe in a grateful breath that you
    sit here
this moment of your life
safely, and in silence.

There is a war raging,
far from this place of comfort.
We know it is there, we know our
    brothers and sisters
suffer its poisonous touch.
Our hearts are weighted with what we
    cannot resolve.
So here we lift a banner in our own
    souls,
and remember that in this place, in this
    moment,
we are not at war.

Breathe in the truth of this moment:
here is our strength, our deep well of
    courage.

Breathing in, we rest our spirits.
Breathing out, we pray for peace.

May those in harm's way be safe
for another day.
May those who drive the engines of
    power
be awakened by compassion.

May we all hold the cup filled with
    courage and will
that has been carried by peacemakers
    in long ages
before us.
May we drink of it deeply, and be
    steadfast
in the ways of peace.

KATHLEEN MCTIGUE, ADAPTED

216

Hay tantísimas fronteras
que dividen a la gente,
pero por cada frontera
existe también un Puente.

There are so many borders
that divide people,
but for every border
there is also a bridge.

GINA VALDÉS,
ENGLISH TRANSLATION BY
KATHERINE CALLEN KING

217

But peace, like a poem,
is not there ahead of itself,
can't be imagined before it is made,
can't be known except
in the words of its making,
grammar of justice,
syntax of mutual aid.

A feeling towards it,
dimly sensing a rhythm, is all we have
Until we begin to utter its metaphors,
learning them as we speak.

A line of peace might appear
if we restructured the sentence our
  lives are making,
revoked its affirmation of profit and
  power,
questioned our needs, allowed
long pauses. . . .

A cadence of peace might balance its
  weight
on that different fulcrum; peace, a
  presence,
an energy field more intense than war,
might pulse then,
stanza by stanza into the world,
each act of living
one of its words, each word
a vibration of light—facets
of the forming crystal.

DENISE LEVERTOV, ADAPTED

218

As we face a troubled and puzzled
  world,
we too are troubled and puzzled.
As our fond dreams remain unrealized
and our bright hopes of yesterday
  wither
in the bitter disappointments of
  today,
our courage fails, our spirits droop,
  our faith trembles,
and, frustrated, we bow our heads
  in despair.

Nevertheless, we come to God in
  this hour of worship, in this house
  of prayer.

As we pray for peace in our time,
  O God,
may we ourselves be at peace with
  the world, with ourselves, and with
  Thee.
May we know that without love there
  will never be peace.
Teach us therefore to love.

EGBERT ETHELRED BROWN

219

O God about whom we know so
  little, but ask so much,
Goddess of Justice, giver and
  sustainer of all Life:

Your daughters and sons call upon
  you once again

as we did in centuries past.
We have known war, and once again,
   there are rumors of wars.
And so we come this morning
to lay this burden on the altar of
   prayer.

We know that violence cannot sustain
   us . . .
And so we seek a new way:
a way that leads to peace . . .
a way that leads to the promise of
freedom, justice, and security
for all the peoples of the Earth.

MARJORIE BOWENS-WHEATLEY

220

For the times when I could have
   made peace
with my neighbor but picked a
   quarrel, forgive me;
and forgive me, too,
for the time when I could have
   accepted with grace
an offering of friendship or
   reconciliation
but did not choose to listen.
At times, in my willfulness,
I may have closed my heart to
the possibility of a healing word:
Today—and tomorrow—
let my heart be open.

CHAIM STERN

221

I am so tired and weary,
   So tired of the endless fight,
So weary of waiting the dawn
   And finding endless night.

That I ask but rest and quiet—
   Rest for the days that are gone,
And quiet for the little space
   That I must journey on.

JOSEPH SEAMON COTTER

222

Let the glory of all life be extolled,
   let creation be hallowed,
In the world whose creation
   surrounds us.
May one world soon prevail,
In our own day,
our own lives,
and the lives of all who live,
and let us say: *Amen.*
Let all life be blessed,
as all life is glorified, exalted,
and honored, beyond all the praises,
   songs, and
adorations that we can utter. The
   world is a wonder beyond our
   understanding,
and let us say: *Amen.*
For us and for all nature,
may the blessing of peace
and the promise of life come true,
and let us say: *Amen.*

May peace reign in the highest and
    lowest places,
let peace descend upon us all
and all the world, and let us say:
    Amen

KADDISH, ADAPTED BY
JULIE ANN SILBERMAN-BUN

223

We pledge to walk together
in the ways of truth and affection,
as best we know them now
or may learn them in days to come,
that we and our children may be
    fulfilled
and that we may speak to the world
in words and actions
of peace and goodwill.

ALICE BLAIR WESLEY

224

May good befall all.

May there be peace for all.

May all be fit for excellence.

May all experience the holy.

May all be happy.

May all be healthy.

May all experience what is good.

May no one suffer.

HINDU PRAYER, TRANSLATED BY
ABHI JANAMANCH, ADAPTED

225

May Divine Mystery protect us
    together.

May God nourish us together.

May we work together uniting our
    strength for the good of humanity.

*May our learning be luminous and
    purposeful.*

May we love one another.

*May there be peace, peace, and perfect
    peace.*

TAITTIRYA UPANISHAD,
TRANSLATED BY ABHI JANAMANCHI,
ADAPTED

226

You and I
Have so much love,
That it
Burns like a fire,
In which we bake a lump of clay
Molded into a figure of you
And a figure of me.

Then we take both of them,

And break them into pieces,

And mix the pieces with water,

And mold again a figure of you,
And a figure of me.

I am in your clay.

You are in my clay.
In life we share a single quilt.
In death we will share one coffin.

KUAN TAO-SHÊNG,
TRANSLATED BY
KENNETH REXROTH AND
LING CHUNG, ADAPTED

227

In the name of the daybreak
and the eyelids of morning
and the wayfaring moon
and the night when it departs.

I swear I will not dishonor
my soul with hatred,
but offer myself humbly
as a guardian of nature,
as a healer of misery,
as a messenger of wonder,
as an architect of peace.

DIANE ACKERMAN

228

There are those who are trying
to set fire to the world.

We are in danger.

There is time only to work slowly.

There is no time not to love.

DEENA METZGER

229

Peace is not the product of terror or
    fear.

Peace is not the silence of cemeteries.

Peace is not the silent result of violent
    repression.

*Peace is the generous, tranquil
    contribution of all
to the good of all.*

Peace is dynamism.

Peace is generosity.

It is right

and it is duty.

OSCAR ROMERO, ADAPTED

230

Spirit of Life
whom we have called by many names
in thanksgiving and in anguish—

*Bless the poets and those who mourn
Send peace for the soldiers who did not
    make the wars
but whose lives were consumed by them*

Let strong trees grow above graves
    far from home
Breathe through the arms of their
    branches
The earth will swallow your tears
    while the dead sing
"No more, never again, remember
    me."

For the wounded ones, and those who
received them back,
let there be someone ready when the
memories come
when the scars pull and the buried
metal moves
and forgiveness for those of us who were
not there
for our ignorance.

And in us, veterans in a forest of a
thousand fallen promises,
let new leaves of protest grow on our
stumps.
Give us courage to answer the cry of
humanity's pain
And with our bare hands, out of full
hearts,
with all our intelligence
let us create the peace.

BARBARA J. PESCAN, ADAPTED

231

Where the mind is without fear and
the head is held high;

Where knowledge is free;

Where the world has not been broken
up into fragments
by narrow domestic walls;

Where words come out from the depth
of truth;

Where tireless striving stretches its
arms towards perfection;

Where the clear stream of reason has not
lost its way into the
dreary desert sand of dead habit;

Where the mind is led forward into
ever-widening
thought and action—

Into that heaven of freedom, let our
country awake.

RABINDRANATH TAGORE, ADAPTED

232

Deliver me to myself
that I may stop fretting the hours
in vain,
looking for what's lacking
always elsewhere and otherwise.
Let befall me the peace
which drops like the wind,
suddenly, between even the slightest
folds of a linnet's wing,
between shadow and sky, the hush
like the intervals of quiet
between questions, between the calls
of crickets, the sorrow
of one season and the next
swift and sure and sharp
as grace.

KATHERINE MOSBY

233

Give us a peace equal to the war

Or else our souls will be unsatisfied,
And we will wonder what we have
* fought for*
And why the many died.

Give us a peace accepting every
  challenge—

The challenge of the poor, the black, of
* all denied,*
The challenge of the vast colonial world
That long has had so little justice by its
* side.*

Give us a peace that dares us to be
  wise,

Give us a peace that dares us to be
* strong.*

Give us a peace that dares us still
  uphold
Throughout the peace our battle
  against wrong.

LANGSTON HUGHES, ADAPTED

234

Eternal wellspring of peace—
may we be drenched with the longing
  for peace
that we may give ourselves over
as the earth to the rain, to the dew,
until peace overflows our lives
as living waters overflow the seas.

MARCIA FALK

235

We have a calling in this world:

We are called to honor diversity,
to respect differences with dignity,
and to challenge those who would
* forbid it.*

We are people of a wide path.

Let us be wide in affection
and go our way in peace.

JEAN M. ROWE

Wisdom

236

Flame, friend of our most ancient
    ancestors,
we kindle you now to make you
    visible in this time.

Yet, in truth, you burn always,

in the unique worth of each person,
in the imagination,

in the turning of the heart to sorrow
    or joy,

in the call to hope
and in the call to justice.
Burn bright before us.

Burn bright within us.

ORLANDA BRUGNOLA

237

We light this chalice

to help us move from untruth to truth,

to help us move from ignorance to
    wisdom,

to help us move from animosity to love,

to help us move from bondage to
    freedom.

We rededicate ourselves before this light
to affirm and practice truth, wisdom,
    love, and freedom
today and in the days to come.

UPANISHADS, ADAPTED

238

We believe—
    that many streams join to make a
    river,
    that the way to wisdom lies in an
    open ear and heart,
    that goodness may be pursued for
    the sake of goodness
    and not from fear of punishment,
    that knowing and not knowing are
    part of the same,
    and ambiguity is permissible.

PATRICK MURFIN

239

Hidden in all stories
is the One story.

The more we listen,
the clearer that story becomes.

Our true identity,
who we are,
why we are here,
what sustains us,

is in this story.

RACHEL NAOMI REMEN, ADAPTED

240

Soy un amasamiento,

I am an act of kneading, of uniting
  and joining,

*that not only has produced both a
  creature of darkness and a creature
  of light,*

but also a creature that questions the
  definitions of light and dark

and gives them new meanings.

GLORIA ANZALDÚA, ADAPTED

241

Have patience with everything
  unresolved in your heart
and to try to love the questions
  themselves

*as if they were locked rooms
or books written in a very foreign
  language.*

Don't search for the answers,
which could not be given to you now,
because you would not be able to live
  them.

And the point is, to live everything.

Live the questions now.

Perhaps then, someday far in the future,

you will gradually, without even
  noticing it,
live your way into the answer.

RAINER MARIA RILKE, TRANSLATED
BY STEPHEN MITCHELL, ADAPTED

242

We have not even to risk the
  adventure alone;

*for the heroes of all time have gone
  before us;*

the labyrinth is thoroughly known;

*we have only to follow the thread of
  the hero path.*

And where we had thought to find
  an abomination,
we shall find a god . . .

*Where we had thought to travel
  outward,*

we will come to the center of our
  own existence;
where we had thought to be alone,
we shall be with all the world.

JOSEPH CAMPBELL, ADAPTED

243

SINGLE VOICE: What can we tell these
  young people of our collective
  wisdom today
  that will help them on their
  journeys?

LEFT: First, be assured that none of
  us knows all the answers
  to the largest questions of our
  existence.
  You will join us in the community
  of doubt, discovery,
  and unfolding truth.

RIGHT: We do know that the gifts of
life are given most richly
to those who embrace the world
with gratitude;
who do their share of humanity's
work cheerfully;
who cherish beauty and simplicity;
who approach their fellow beings
with compassion, patience,
and generosity.

LEFT: We do know that we are called
upon to act with integrity,
and to do good to others,
even when we are weary, or in
need, or misunderstood.
We do know that you must
cultivate your heart,
and educate your conscience,
for in the end you must trust what
they tell you.

ALL: We know that you are each
precious to us,
and that we wish for you all
happiness.
We would have you to know that
our blessing and care
go with you on your journeys,
and we promise you our steadfast
friendship and support.

KENDYL GIBBONS

244

I am afraid of things that cannot
harm me, and I know it.
I yearn for things that cannot help
me, and I know it.

What I fear is within me, and within
me, too, is what I seek.

CHASIDIC PRAYER,
TRANSLATED BY CHAIM STERN

245

What do I want?
And if I want it, do I need it?
And if I need it, will I get it?
And if I get it, can I keep it?
Do the answers depend on who I am?
Help me to be what I am
becoming. . . .
Is that "becoming" more than I am
right now?
Help me to trust the dawning hour.
Help me to know myself better.
Help me to become myself.

CHAIM STERN

246

Amid all the noise in our lives,
we take this moment to sit in
silence—
to give thanks for another day,
to give thanks for all those in our lives
who have brought us warmth and
love,
to give thanks for the gift of life.

*We know we are on our pilgrimage here
but a brief moment in time.*

Let us open ourselves, here, now,
to the process of becoming more
whole—
of living more fully,

of giving and forgiving more freely,
of understanding more completely the
*   meaning of our lives here on this*
*   earth.*

TIMOTHY HALEY

247

As we move through life
finding ourselves,

always newly wise and newly foolish,

we ask that our mistakes be small
and not hurtful.

We ask that as we gain experience

we do not forget our innocence,
for they are both part of the whole.

ORLANDA BRUGNOLA

248

Spirit of Life and Love,
why is there something,
instead of nothing?

Why do wishes sometimes come true,
when spoken beneath the stars?

Why, after millions of years of life
    on this earth,
does death still sting?

Why is it so hard
for people to learn how to love one
*   another?*

Why does my heart laugh
with the first flower of spring?

Questions rise up within our souls,
born of fear and delight,
sorrow and confusion.

Questions live within us,
shaping our choices,
and our search for truth.

Help us to embrace them and to grow.

LISA FRIEDMAN

249

This alone is what I wish for you:
    knowledge.
To understand each desire has an
    edge,
to know we are responsible for the
    lives
we change. No faith comes without
    cost,
no one believes without dying.

RITA DOVE

250

To be strong enough to gain some
    mastery over ourselves
and humble enough to be willing to
    learn from others;

To be brave enough to choose the right
*   road, no matter how hard it may be,*
and patient enough to keep on in spite
*   of obstacles;*

To be wise enough to know our own
    shortcomings
and honest enough to admit the
    excellence of others;

To be proud enough to command the
respect of strong individuals
and gentle enough to win the love of
little children;

To be careful enough to protect the
goods of others
and generous enough to share our
own;

This is our aspiration for today.

GEORGE G. DAVIS

251

This making of a whole self takes
such a very long time: pieces are not
sequential nor our supplies.

We work here, then there,
hold up tattered fabric to the light.
Sew past dark, intent. Use all our
thread.

Sleeves may come before length;
buttons, before a rounded neck.

We sew at what most needs us,
and as it asks, sew again.

The self is not one thing, once made,
unaltered. Not midnight task alone,
not
after other work.

It's everything we come upon, make
ours:
all this fitting of what-once-was and
has-become.

NANCY SHAFFER, ADAPTED

252

When we are feeling confident in our
livelihoods, limited as they are,
remind us, O God, of your unlimited
splendor in the universe.

When we are feeling as though nothing
will limit us, even though we age,
remind us, O God, that our journey
will one day end.

When we are feeling prosperous, even
though we know all we own will
perish,
remind us, O God, that we cannot
take anything with us.

When we are feeling so wise, even
though we know our knowledge is
partial
remind us, O God, that we can't even
know what tomorrow will bring.

When we pat ourselves on the back
for how much we give, even
though it's not so much
remind us, O God, that your
goodness has no bounds.

For we would live without swagger.
We would live with grounded
wisdom.
We would open our hearts to others,
that your light is the glow that
illumines our lives.

ARYANTO NUGROHO

253

Between two words,
choose the quieter one.
Between word and silence,
choose listening.
Between two books,
choose the dustier one.
Between the earth and the sky,
choose a bird.
Between two animals,
choose the one who needs you more.
Between two children,
choose both.
Between the lesser and the bigger evil,
choose neither.
Between hope and despair
choose hope:
it will be harder to bear.

BORIS NOVAK, TRANSLATED BY
MIA DINTINJANA

Acknowledgments

Copyright holders of selections marked with a * have authorized photocopying and livestreaming for worship.

1 Rainer Maria Rilke, translated by Anita Barrows and Joanna Macy. "Du Dunkelheit, aus der . . . /You, darkness, of whom . . . ," from *Rilke's Book of Hours: Love Poems to God* by Rainer Maria Rilke, translated by Anita Barrows and Joanna Macy, translation copyright © 1996 by Anita Barrows and Joanna Macy. Used by permission of Riverhead Books, an imprint of Penguin Group (USA) Inc.

2 Sarah York (Sara Moores Campbell) (UU). From "Give Us the Child" in *Into the Wilderness* (Skinner House Books). *

3 Czesław Milosz. "On Prayer" in *New and Collected Poems: 1931–2000* by Czesław Milosz. Copyright © 1988, 1991, 1995, 2001 by Czesław Milosz Royalties, Inc. Reprinted by permission of HarperCollins Publishers.

4 Lisa Friedman (UU). *

5 Jane Hirshfield. "Autumn" in *The October Palace* by Jane Hirshfield. Copyright © 1994 by Jane Hirshfield. Reprinted by permission of HarperCollins Publishers.

6 Rainer Maria Rilke, translated by Anita Barrows and Joanna Macy. "Da neigt sich die Stunde . . . /The hour is striking . . ." in *Rilke's Book of Hours: Love Poems to God* by Rainer Maria Rilke, translated by Anita Barrows and Joanna Macy, translation copyright © 1996 by Anita Barrows and Joanna Macy. Used by permission of Riverhead Books, an imprint of Penguin Group (USA) Inc.

7 John Soos. In *Earth Prayers: 365 Prayers, Poems, and Invocations from Around the World*, edited by Elizabeth Roberts and Elias Amidon (HarperOne). *

8 Sone No Yoshitada, translated by Kenneth Rexroth. "The lower leaves of the trees" by Sone No Yoshitada, translated by Kenneth Rexroth, in *One Hundred More Poems from the Japanese*, copyright © 1976 by Kenneth Rexroth. Reprinted by permission of New Directions Publishing Corp.

9 Julianne Lepp (UU). *

10 Edna St. Vincent Millay. From "Autumn Chant" in *The Harp Weaver and Other Poems* (Harper Brothers Publishers). *

11 Jalal al-Din Rumi, translated by Coleman Barks. Adapted from "One Song" from *The Soul of Rumi: A New Collection of Ecstatic Poems*, translated by Coleman Barks, HarperCollins, 2003. © Coleman Barks. *

12 Kabir, translated by Rabindranath Tagore. From *Songs of Kabir*, translated by Rabindranath Tagore (Forgotten Books). *

13 Chaim Stern. From *Day by Day* by Chaim Stern. Copyright © 1998 by the Central Conference of American Rabbis. Reprinted by permission of Beacon Press, Boston.

14 Sarah York (Sara Moores Campbell) (UU). "Benediction" in *Into the Wilderness* (Skinner House Books). *

15 Nita Penfold (UU). From *They Stand Up in Broken Shells*. *

16 Nancy Shaffer (UU). "In Stillness" in *Instructions in Joy* (Skinner House Books). *

17 Denise Levertov. "The Avowal" by Denise Levertov, from *Oblique Prayers*, copyright © 1984 by Denise Levertov. Reprinted by permission of New Directions Publishing Corp.

18 Jalal al-Din Rumi, translated by Coleman Barks. Adapted from "Where Everything Is Music" in *The Essential Rumi*, translated by Coleman Barks, HarperCollins, 1995. © Coleman Barks. *

19 Gordon B. McKeeman (UU). In 1997 Worship Materials Collection (Unitarian Universalist Ministers Association). *

20 Amanda Udis-Kessler (UU). *

21 Sarum Primer. In *Bless All Who Serve: Sources of Hope, Courage and Faith for Military Personnel and Their Families*, edited by Matthew and Gail Tittle (Skinner House Books). *

22 Marta I. Valentín (UU).

23 Jonipher Kwong (UU). "Our Voices Must Be Heard" from *Voices from the Margins* (Skinner House Books). *

24 Kathleen McTigue (UU). From "Sabbath Home" in *Shine and Shadow* (Skinner House Books). *

25 Kathleen McTigue (UU). From "Sabbath Home" in *Shine and Shadow* (Skinner House Books). *

26 Wendy Bartel and Lynn Gardner (UU). *

27 Katherine HawkerSelf. From "Come as You Are" from www.liturgyoutside.net.

28 Barbara J. Pescan (UU). From "Prayer for Those Gathered in Worship" in *Morning Watch* (Skinner House Books). *

29 Kathleen McTigue (UU). From "You Who Are Broken Hearted" in *Shine and Shadow* (Skinner House Books). *

30 John Gibb Millspaugh (UU). *

31 Martha Kirby Capo (UU) *

32 Bernadette R. Burns (UU). *

33 Patrick Murfin (UU). From "We Gather as Leaders" in *We Build Temples in the Heart: Side by Side We Gather* (Skinner House Books). *

34 Elizabeth Tarbox (UU). From "Ours Is a Story of Faith" in *Evening Tide* (Skinner House Books).

35 Sobonfu Somé. From *The Spirit of Intimacy: Ancient Teachings in the Ways of Relationships* (HarperCollins). *

36 Starhawk (UU). From *Dreaming the Dark: Magic, Sex, and Politics* (Beacon Press). *

37 Jim Scott (UU). SATB choral arrangement available from jimscottmusic.com. *

38 Leslie Takahashi (UU). *

39 A. Powell Davies (Unitarian). From "When Two Individuals Come Together" in *Great Occasions*, edited by Carl Seaburg (Skinner House). *

40 Pamela Rumancik (UU). *

41 Penny Hackett-Evans (UU).

42 Kathy Huff (UU). *

43 Thomas Merton. From *Conjectures of a Guilty Bystander* (Doubleday). *

44 Alfred A. Duckett. From "Sonnet" in *The Poetry of the Negro*, edited by Langston Hughes and Arna Bontemps (Doubleday). *

45 Hillel. From Pirkei Avot 1:14 from *The Life and Teachings of Hillel* by Yitzhak Buxbaum (Rowman & Littlefield). *

46 Nelson Mandela. From *Long Walk to Freedom: The Autobiography of Nelson Mandela* (Little, Brown & Co.). *

47 Rebecca Ann Parker (UU). From *Blessing the World: What Can Save Us Now*, edited by Rob Hardies. *

48 Stephen Kendrick (UU). *

49 Samir Selmanovic. From *It's Really All About God: Reflections of a Muslim Atheist Jewish Christian* (Jossey Bass). *

50 Christian de la Huerta. From "We Must Shine" from *Soulful Power*, http://www .soulfulpower.com/blog/we-must-shine/. Reprinted by permission of the author.

51 Clyde Grubbs (UU). *

52 Martin Luther King Jr. Adapted from *Thou, Dear God* by Martin Luther King Jr. Reprinted by arrangement with The Heirs to the Estate of Martin Luther King Jr., c/o Writers House as agent for the proprietor, New York, NY. Copyright © 2012 by the Family of Dr. Martin Luther King Jr.

53 Martha Kirby Capo (UU). *

54 Howard Thurman. From "I Confess" in *Meditations of the Heart*. Copyright © 1953, 1981 by Anne Thurman. Reprinted by permission of Beacon Press, Boston.

55 Jane Ellen Mauldin (UU). From "Prayer for Faith" in *Glory, Hallelujah! Now Please Pick Up Your Socks* (Skinner House Books). *

56 Barnaby Feder (UU). *

57 Martha Kirby Capo (UU). *

58 Alfred, Lord Tennyson. From "Ulysses" in *Poems*, vol. 2, edited by Edward Moxon (1842).

59 Martin Luther King Jr. "Toward the Promised Land" from *Thou, Dear God* by Martin Luther King Jr. Reprinted by arrangement with The Heirs to the Estate of Martin Luther King Jr., c/o Writers House as agent for the proprietor, New York, NY. Copyright © 2012 by the Family of Dr. Martin Luther King Jr.

60 Kahlil Gibran. From "On Work" from *The Prophet* by Kahlil Gibran, copyright 1923 by Kahlil Gibran and renewed 1951 by

Administrators C.T.A. of Kahlil Gibran Estate and Mary G. Gibran. Used by permission of Alfred A. Knopf, a division of Random House, Inc.

61 Joy Harjo. From "Reconciliation: A Prayer" in *The Woman Who Fell from the Sky* by Joy Harjo. Copyright © 1994 by Joy Harjo. Used by permission of W.W. Norton & Company, Inc.

62 Aryanto Nugroho (Unitarian). *

63 Langston Hughes. "Youth" from *The Collected Poems of Langston Hughes* by Langston Hughes, edited by Arnold Rampersad with David Roessel, Associate Editor, copyright © 1994 by the Estate of Langston Hughes. Used by permission of Alfred A. Knopf, an imprint of the Knopf Doubleday Publishing Group, a division of Penguin Random House LLC. All rights reserved.

64 Jill Ann Terwilliger (UU). *

65 Gates of Repentance. From *Day by Day* by Chaim Stern. Copyright © 1998 by the Central Conference of American Rabbis. Reprinted by permission of Beacon Press, Boston.

66 Wisława Szymborska, translated by Stanisław Baranczak and Clare Cavanagh. Excerpt from "A Note" from *Monologue of a Dog: New Poems* by Wisława Szymborska, translated from the Polish by Stanisław Baranczak and Clare Cavanagh. Copyright © 2002 by Wisława Szymborska. English translation copyright © 2006 by Houghton Mifflin Harcourt Publishing Company. Reprinted by permission of Houghton Mifflin Harcourt Publishing Company. All rights reserved.

67 Leslie Takahashi (UU). *

68 Annie Dillard. From *Holy the Firm* (Harper & Row). *

69 Galway Kinnell. "A Prayer" from *The Past* by Galway Kinnell. Copyright © 1985 by Galway Kinnell. Reprinted by permission of Houghton Mifflin Harcourt Publishing Company. All rights reserved.

70 Susan Manker-Seale (UU). From "Benediction" in *Awakened from the Forest: Meditations on Ministry*, collected by Gary E. Smith (Skinner House Books).

71 Malka Heifetz Tussman, translated by Marcia Falk. Adapted from "Leaves" from *With Teeth in the Earth: Selected Poems of Malka Heifetz Tussman* translated by Marcia Falk. Copyright © 1992 Wayne State University Press, with the permission of Wayne State University Press.

72 George Campbell. From "Litany" in *First Poems* by George Campbell, City Printery, 1945. Reprinted by permission of Christine and Marion Campbell. *

73 Jim Scott (UU). SATB choral arrangement available from jimscottmusic.com. *

74 Bernadette R. Burns (UU). *

75 William Stafford. Excerpt from "You Reading This, Be Ready" from *The Way It Is: New and Selected Poems*. Copyright © 1998 by the Estate of William Stafford. Reprinted with the permission of The Permissions Company, Inc., on behalf of Graywolf Press, www.graywolfpress.org.

76 Francisco X. Alarcón. From "In Ixtli In Yollotl/Face and Heart" from *The Other Side of Night/Del otro lado de la noche: New and Selected Poems*, by Francisco X. Alarcón. © 2002 Francisco X. Alarcón. Reprinted by permission of the University of Arizona Press.

77 Charles Enoch Wheeler. From "Adjuration" in *The Poetry of the Negro*, edited by Langston Hughes and Arna Bontemps (Doubleday). *

78 Robert Frost. From "Two Tramps in Mud Time" in *The Poetry of Robert Frost* edited by Edward Connery Lathem, copyright © 1923, 1969 by Henry Holt and Company, copyright © 1951 by Robert Frost, reprinted by permission of Henry Holt and Company LLC, all rights reserved.

79 Robert Frost. "Nothing Gold Can Stay" in *The Poetry of Robert Frost* edited by Edward Connery Lathem, copyright © 1923, 1969 by Henry Holt and Company, copyright © 1951 by Robert Frost, reprinted by permission of Henry Holt and Company LLC, all rights reserved.

80 Kathleen Raine. From "Spell Against Sorrow," copyright © 2001 by Kathleen Raine, from *The Collected Poems of Kathleen Raine*. Reprinted by permission of Counterpoint.

81 Stephen Levine. From "There Is an Elemental Love" in *Breaking the Drought, Visions of Grace*, reprinted by permission of Larson Publications.

82 Wisława Szymborska, translated by Stanisław Barańczak and Clare Cavanagh. Excerpt from "A Few Words on the Soul" in *Monologue of a Dog: New Poems by Wisława Szymborska*, translated from the Polish by Stanisław Barańczak and Clare Cavanagh. Copyright © 2002 by Wisława Szymborska. English translation copyright © 2006 by Houghton Mifflin Harcourt Publishing Company. Reprinted by permission of Houghton Mifflin Harcourt Publishing Company. All rights reserved.

83 Parker J. Palmer. In *Peace Prayers: Meditations, Affirmations, Invocations, Poems, and Prayers for Peace*, ed. Carrie Leadingham, Joanne E. Moschella, & Hilary M. Vartanian, HarperSanFrancisco, 1992. Learn more about Parker J. Palmer at www.CourageRenewal.org.

84 Gary Kowalski (UU). In *Rejoice Together: Prayers, Meditations and Other Readings for Family, Individual, and Small Group Worship*, edited by Helen Pickett (Skinner House Books). *

85 Mark Ward (UU). *

86 Mark Ward (UU). *

87 Lois E. Van Leer (UU). *

88 Brian Kiely (UU). *

89 Albert Camus, translated by Justin O'Brien. From *Resistance, Rebellion, and Death: Essays*, translated by Justin O'Brien (Alfred A. Knopf). *

90 Anne Frank. Excerpt from *The Diary of Anne Frank* in *Day by Day*, edited by Chaim Stern (Beacon Press). *

91 Rainer Maria Rilke, translated by Jessie Lamont. "Autumn" from *Poems*, translated by Jessie Lamont (Tobias A. Wright). *

92 Shu Ting, translated by Carolyn Kizer. Adapted from Shu Ting, "Perhaps . . . ," translated by Carolyn Kizer, from *Cool, Calm, & Collected: Poems 1960–2000*. Copyright © 2001 by Carolyn Kizer. Reprinted with the permission of The Permissions Company, Inc., on behalf of Copper Canyon Press, www.coppercanyonpress.org.

93 John A. Buehrens (UU) and Rebecca Ann Parker (UU). From *A House for Hope: The Promise of Progressive Religion for the Twenty-First Century* (Beacon Press). *

94 Jeanne Harrison Nieuwejaar (UU). From *Fluent in Faith: A Unitarian Universalist Embrace of Religious Language* (Skinner House). *

95 Carl Sandburg. From "At a Window" in *Chicago Poems* (Henry Holt & Co.). *

96 Angela Herrera (UU). "Prayer for Travelers" in *Reaching for the Sun* (Skinner House Books). *

97 Angela Herrera (UU). "Oración para los Viajeros," in *Reaching for the Sun* (Skinner House Books). *

98 M. Susan Milnor (UU). *

99 Lisa Friedman (UU). *

100 Maureen Killoran (UU). *

101 June Jordan. From "Old Stories: New Lives" in *Moving Towards Home: Political Essays* (Virago). *

102 Jalal al-Din Rumi, translated by Coleman Barks. From "Where Everything Is Music" from *The Essential Rumi*, tr. Coleman Barks, HarperCollins, 1995. © Coleman Barks. *

103 Margaret Williams Braxton (UU). From "Some Day" in *Been in the Storm So Long*, edited by Mark D. Morrison-Reed and Jacqui James (Skinner House Books). *

104 David Maywhoor (UU). *

105 Yehuda Amichai, translated by Stephen Mitchell. Adapted from "The Place Where We Are Right" from *The Selected Poetry of Yehuda Amichai*, tr. Stephen Mitchell, HarperCollins, 1986. Reprinted by permission of the Copyright Clearance Center.

106 Langston Hughes. "Dusk" from *The Collected Poems of Langston Hughes* by Langston Hughes, edited by Arnold Rampersad with David Roessel, Associate Editor, copyright © 1994 by the Estate of Langston Hughes. Used by permission of Alfred A. Knopf, an imprint of the Knopf Doubleday Publishing Group, a division of Penguin Random House LLC. All rights reserved.

107 Maureen Killoran (UU). *

108 David Blanchard (UU). *

109 Matt Meyer (UU). *

110 Angela Herrera (UU). From "Invocation" in *Reaching for the Sun* (Skinner House Books). *

111 Petr Samojsky (Unitarian). *

112 Beverly Bumbaugh (UU) and David Bumbaugh (UU). *

113 Forrest Church (UU). From *A Chosen Faith: An Introduction to Unitarian Universalism* by Forrest Church and John A. Buehrens (Beacon Press). *

114 June Jordan. From "These Poems" in *Directed by Desire: The Collected Poems of June Jordan* (2005). © 2013 June Jordan Literary Estate. Reprinted by permission. www.junejordan.com.

115 Nikki Giovanni. Excerpt from "Swaziland" ["I am old and need/ . . . will you remember the music."] in *Love Poems* by Nikki Giovanni. Copyright © 1968–1997 by Nikki Giovanni. Reprinted by permission of HarperCollins Publishers.

116 Allison Joseph. Excerpt from "On Being Told I Don't Speak Like a Black Person" from *Imitation of Life*. Copyright © 2003 by Allison Joseph. Reprinted with the permission of The Permissions Company, Inc., on behalf of Carnegie Mellon University Press, www.cmu.edu/universitypress.

117 Galway Kinnell. Excerpt from "Saint Francis and the Sow" in *Mortal Acts, Mortal Words* by Galway Kinnell. Copyright © 1980, renewed 2008 by Galway Kinnell. Reprinted by permission of Houghton Mifflin Harcourt Publishing Company. All rights reserved.

118 Irena Klepfisz. Adapted from Dedications to "*Bashert*" by Irena Klepfisz, © 1990 by Irena Klepfisz, in *A Few Words in the Mother Tongue: Poems Selected and New (1971–1990)* (Portland, OR: The Eighth Mountain Press, 1990), © 1990 by Irena Klepfisz. Reprinted by permission of the author and publisher. *

119 Irena Klepfisz. Adapted from Dedications to "*Bashert*" by Irena Klepfisz, © 1990 by Irena Klepfisz, in *A Few Words in the Mother Tongue: Poems Selected and New (1971–1990)* (Portland, OR: The Eighth Mountain Press, 1990). © 1990 by Irena Klepfisz. Reprinted by permission of the author and publisher. *

120 Erika Hewitt (UU). *

121 Amy Carol Webb (UU). *

122 Fulgence Ndagijamana (UU). *

123 Rolf Jacobsen, translated by Robert Hedin. Adapted from "When They Sleep" by Rolf Jacobsen, translated by Robert Hedin, from *The Roads Have Come to an End Now: Selected and Last Poems of Rolf Jacobsen* (Port Townsend, Washington: Copper Canyon Press, 2001). Reprinted by permission of Robert Hedin. *

124 Derek Walcott. "Love after Love" from *The Poetry of Derek Walcott, 1948–2013* by Derek Walcott, selected by Glyn Maxwell. Copyright © 2014 by Derek Walcott. Reprinted by permission of Farrar, Straus, and Giroux, LLC.

125 Betsy Darr (UU). *

126 Bettye A. Doty (UU). *

127 Joy Harjo. From "Finding the Groove" in *Word: On Being a [Woman] Writer*, edited by Jocelyn Burrell (Feminist Press). *

128 William Schulz (UU). In *Welcome: A Unitarian Universalist Primer*, edited by Patricia Frevert (Skinner House Books). *

129 Aaron R. Payson (UU). From "Mealtime" in *Everyday Spiritual Practice*, edited by Scott Alexander (Skinner House Books). *

130 Elizabeth Tarbox (UU). From the Preface to *Life Tides* (Skinner House Books). Reprinted by permission of Sarah Tarbox.

131 Billy Collins. Excerpt from "Directions" in *The Art of Drowning* by Billy Collins, © 1995. Reprinted by permission of the University of Pittsburgh Press.

132 Gary Kowalski (UU). *

133 Pierre Teilhard de Chardin. In *Peace Prayers: Meditations, Affirmations, Invocations, Poems and Prayers for Peace*, edited by Carrie Leadingham (HarperOne). *

134 Václav Havel. From "The World in Our Hands," Harvard commencement speech, June 8, 1995, in *Sunrise Magazine*, October/November 1995 (Theosophical University Press, www.theosophy-nw.org/theosnw/issues/gl-hav2.htm). *

135 Kenneth Patton (UU). From "The Human Condition" in *The Sense of Life* (Meeting House Press). Reprinted by permission of Clarise Patton. *

136 Walt Whitman. From *Leaves of Grass* (1882). *

137 Kendyl Gibbons (UU). *

138 Addae Ama Kraba (UU). *

139 Langston Hughes. From "Earth Song" in *The Collected Poems of Langston Hughes* by Langston Hughes, edited by Arnold Rampersad with David Roessel, Associate

Editor, copyright © 1994 by the Estate of Langston Hughes. Used by permission of Alfred A. Knopf, a division of Random House, Inc.

140 Navajo chant. "A Prayer of the Night Chant" in *Native American Traditions*, edited by Sam Gill (Wadsworth Publishing). *

141 Joy Harjo. Adapted from "Remember," copyright © 1983 by Joy Harjo, from *She Had Some Horses* by Joy Harjo. Used by permission of W.W. Norton & Company, Inc.

142 Rig Veda. "Let Us Be United" from *Rig Veda*, at *World Prayers*, www.worldprayers.org. *

143 Barbara Deming. From "Spirit of Love" in *We Are All Part of One Another: A Barbara Deming Reader* (New Society Publishers).

144 Rosemary Bray McNatt (UU). Permission granted to photocopy for one-time use in worship. *

145 Mahatma Gandhi. From "Discussion with Teacher" in *Harijan*, September 5, 1936. *

146 Aung San Suu Kyi. From "Freedom from Fear" in *Freedom from Fear and Other Writings*, edited by Michael Aris (Penguin Group). *

147 W.S. Merwin. "Daybreak" by W.S. Merwin. Currently collected in *Second Four Books of Poems* by W.S. Merwin. Copyright © 1993 by W.S. Merwin. Used by permission of The Wylie Agency LLC.

148 Simon Ortiz. From *Sand Creek*. Copyright © 1993 Simon Ortiz. Reprinted by permission of Avalon Travel, a member of the Perseus Books Group.

149 Martin Luther King Jr. From "Where Do We Go From Here" in *A Testament of Hope: The Essential Writings and Speeches of Martin Luther King, Jr.*, edited by James M. Washington (HarperCollins). *

150 William Schulz (UU). From *Engagement with the World* (Unitarian Universalist Association). *

151 Nelson Mandela. From inauguration speech, Pretoria, May 10, 1994, in "Mandela—In His Own Words: Quotations from Nelson Mandela's Best-Known Speeches and Statements," *The Observer*, February 10, 2001, www.guardian.co.uk/world/2001/feb/11/nelsonmandela.southafrica. *

152 Maya Angelou. From *On the Pulse of Morning* by Maya Angelou, copyright © 1993 by Maya Angelou. Used by permission of Random House, Inc.

153 Audre Lorde. From "On My Way Out I Passed Over You and the Verrazano Bridge," in *Our Dead Behind Us* by Audre Lorde. Copyright © 1986 by Audre Lorde. Used by permission of W.W. Norton & Company, Inc.

154 Wendy Bartel (UU). "Border Crossings." *

155 Christine Robinson (UU). *

156 Ken Collier (UU). *

157 Paul N. Carnes (UU). In *Longing of the Heart: Prayers and Invocations* (Unitarian Universalist Association). *

158 Martin Luther King, Jr. From *A Testament of Hope* (HarperCollins).

159 William Sinkford (UU). *

160 Debra Faulk (UU). *

161 Marta I. Valentín (UU).

162 Marta I. Valentín (UU), translated by Maria Cristina Vlassidis Burgoa (UU) and Iréne Durand Bryan.

163 Barbara Merritt (UU). "Welcome" wallet card (Unitarian Universalist Association). *

164 David Bumbaugh (UU). *

165 Lewis A. McGee (Unitarian). From "We May Have It!" in *Been in the Storm So Long*, edited by Mark Morrison-Reed and Jacqui James (Skinner House Books). *

166 James Luther Adams (UU). From "The Chief End of Human Existence" in *An Examined Faith: Social Context and Religious Commitment* by James Luther Adams, edited by George K. Beach (Beacon Press). *

167 Edward L. Schempp (UU), from "Conspiracy with Change" in *UU World*, www.uuworld.org/2004/02/heritage.html. *

168 Aisha Hauser (UU) and Susan Lawrence (UU). From *Wonderful Welcome: A Tapestry of Faith Program for Children* (Unitarian Universalist Association), www.uua.org/re/tapestry/children/welcome/index.shtml. *

169 Kendyl Gibbons (UU). *

170 Mark Belletini (UU), inspired by David Richo, *The Five Things We Cannot Change: And the Happiness We Find by Embracing Them* (Shambhala Publications). *

171 Mark Belletini (UU). From "In Heaven" in *Sonata for Voice and Silence* (Skinner House Books). *

172 Edward Searl (UU). From *We Pledge Our Hearts: A Treasury of Poems, Quotations and Readings to Celebrate Love and Marriage*, edited by Edward Searl (Skinner House Books). *

173 George Eliot. From *Middlemarch: A Study of Provincial Life* (1874). *

174 Tim O'Brien. From "Spin" in *The Things They Carried* (Mariner Books). *

175 Alice Walker. Excerpt from "In These Dissenting Times" from *Revolutionary Petunias & Other Poems* by Alice Walker. Copyright © 1970, and renewed 1998 by Alice Walker. Reprinted by permission of Houghton Mifflin Harcourt Publishing Company. All rights reserved.

176 Lynn Gardner (UU). *

177 Adapted by Roger Jones (UU). *

178 Kendyl Gibbons (UU). *

179 Mark Belletini (UU). *

180 Leslie Takahashi (UU). *

181 Judith Meyer (UU). From "To Live in This World," the sermon for the Service of the Living Tradition, Unitarian Universalist Association General Assembly, 2006. *

182 Barbara Rohde (UU). From "A Collaborative Effort" in *In the Simple Morning Light* (Skinner House Books). *

183 John B. Wolf (UU). *

184 Rebecca Ann Parker (UU). From "What They Dreamed Be Ours to Do" in *Redeeming Time: Endowing Your Church with the Power of Covenant*, edited by Walter P. Herz (Skinner House Books). *

185 Maya Angelou. From *Love's Exquisite Freedom* (Welcome Enterprises).

186 James Baldwin. From *Nothing Personal* by James Baldwin and Richard Avedon (Penguin). *

187 Patrick Murfin (UU). From "Merlin Said," in *We Build Temples in the Heart: Side by Side We Gather* (Skinner House Books). *

188 Dinah Maria Mulock Craik. From *A Life for a Life* (1859). *

189 Antonio Machado, translated by Alan S. Trueblood. "Has my heart gone to sleep?" Reprinted by permission of the publisher from *Antonio Machado: Selected Poems*, translated by Alan S. Trueblood, p. 93, Cambridge, MA: Harvard University Press, copyright © 1982 by the President and Fellows of Harvard College.

190 Antonio Machado. "¿Mi corazón se ha dormido?" from *Times Alone: Selected Poems of Antonio Machado* © Antonio Machado, translation © 1983 by Robert Bly. Reprinted by permission of Wesleyan University Press. *

191 Steve Abbott. From "Hit by a Space Station" in *Stretching the Agape Bra* (Androgyne Press). Reprinted by permission of Alysia Abbott. *

192 Robert R. Walsh (UU). From "Fault Line" from *Noisy Stones* (Skinner House Books). *

193 Jan Carlsson-Bull (UU). "Love and Loving," in *We Pledge Our Hearts: A Treasury of Poems, Quotations and Readings to Celebrate Love and Marriage*, edited by Edward Searl (Skinner House Books). *

194 Emily Dickinson. From "Love" in *Poems, Third Series* (1896). *

195 W.M. Vories. In *Day by Day*, edited by Chaim Stern (Beacon Press). *

196 Rebecca Ann Parker (UU). From *Blessing the World: What Can Save Us Now* by Rebecca Ann Parker, edited by Robert Hardies (Skinner House Books). *

197 Kendyl Gibbons (UU). *

198 Richard S. Gilbert (UU). From "We Are, Therefore We Love," in *In the Holy Quiet of This Hour* (Skinner House Books). *

199 Audre Lorde. From "If You Come Softly." Copyright © 1968 by Audre Lorde, from *The Collected Poems of Audre Lorde* by Audre Lorde. Used by permission of W.W. Norton & Company, Inc.

200 Archibald MacLeish. From "Psyche with the Candle" from *Collected Poems, 1917–1982* by Archibald MacLeish. Copyright © 1985 by The Estate of Archibald MacLeish. Reprinted by permission of Houghton Mifflin Harcourt Publishing Company. All rights reserved.

201 Alice Walker. From *Hard Times Require Furious Dancing*. Copyright © 2010 by Alice Walker. Reprinted with permission from New World Library, Novato, CA. www.newworldlibrary.com. *

202 Mark Belletini (UU). "Love Prayer" in *Sonata for Voice and Silence* (Skinner House Books). *

203 Barbara Hamilton-Holway (UU). "Go Now in Peace" in *We Pledge Our Hearts: A Treasury of Poems, Quotations, and Readings*

to Celebrate Love and Marriage, edited by
Edward Searl (Skinner House Books). *

204 John Morgan (UU). Permission granted to
photocopy for one-time use in worship.

205 Carl Sandburg. From "Let Love Go On" in
Smoke and Steel (Harcourt, Brace & Co.). *

206 Brian Kiely (UU). *

207 Barbara J. Pescan (UU). From "Love
Abides" in Morning Watch (Skinner House
Books). *

208 Edna St. Vincent Millay. From "Druid's
Chant" in Collected Poems (HarperCollins). *

209 Wayne B. Arnason (UU). *

210 Rainer Maria Rilke, translated by Anita
Barrows and Joanna Macy. "Alles wird
wieder gross . . . /All will come again into
its strength," from Rilke's Book of Hours:
Love Poems to God by Rainer Maria Rilke,
translated by Anita Barrows and Joanna
Macy, translation copyright © 1996 by
Anita Barrows and Joanna Macy. Used by
permission of Riverhead Books, an imprint
of Penguin Group (USA) Inc.

211 Owen Dodson. From "The Decision" in
The Poetry of the Negro, edited by Langston
Hughes and Arna Bontemps (Doubleday). *

212 Tim O'Brien. From "How to Tell a War
Story" in The Things They Carried (Mariner
Books). *

213 Qur'an 25:63, translated by Abdullah Yusuf
Ali. From The Holy Qur'an, translated by
Abdullah Yusuf Ali (Wordsworth Editions). *

214 Max Warren. From Introduction to The
Primal Vision: Christian Presence Amid
African Religion by John V. Taylor (Fortress
Press). *

215 Kathleen McTigue (UU). From "Breathing
Peace into Being" in Shine and Shadow
(Skinner House Books). *

216 Gina Valdés, English translation by
Katherine Callen King. "Copla #1," from
Puentes y fronteras/Bridges and Borders,
translated by Katherine Callen King, ©
Bilingual Press/Editorial Bilingüe (Arizona
State University, Tempe, AZ).

217 Denise Levertov. From "Making Peace"
in Breathing the Water, copyright ©
1987 by Denise Levertov. Reprinted by
permission of New Directions Publishing
Corp.

218 Egbert Ethelred Brown (Unitarian). From
"Without Love" in Been in the Storm So

Long, edited by Mark Morrison-Reed and
Jacqui James (Skinner House Books). *

219 Marjorie Bowens-Wheatley (UU). From
prayer delivered at Fourth Universalist
Society in New York, NY, "Unitarian
Universalist Perspectives: Liturgical
Elements: The War Against Iraq." Reprinted
by permission of Clyde Grubbs. *

220 Chaim Stern. From Day by Day. Copyright
© 1998 by the Central Conference of
American Rabbis. Reprinted by permission
of Beacon Press, Boston.

221 Joseph Seamon Cotter. "Supplication" in
The Band of Gideon and Other Lyrics (The
Cornhill Co.). *

222 Kaddish, adapted by Julie Ann Silberman-
Bun (UU). *

223 Alice Blair Wesley (UU). From Our
Covenant: The 2000–01 Minns Lectures:
The Lay and Liberal Doctrine of the Church:
The Spirit and Promise of Our Covenant
(Meadville Lombard Theological School
Press). *

224 Traditional Hindu prayer, translated by
Abhi Janamanchi (UU). *

225 Taittirya Upanishad, translated by Abhi
Janamanchi (UU). *

226 Kuan Tao-shêng, translated by Kenneth
Rexroth and Ling Chung. In Women Poets
of China, copyright © 1973 by Kenneth
Rexroth and Ling Chung. Reprinted by
permission of New Directions Publishing
Corp.

227 Diane Ackerman. "School Prayer," from
I Praise My Destroyer by Diane Ackerman,
copyright © 1998 by Diane Ackerman.
Used by permission of Random House, Inc.

228 Deena Metzger. From "Song" in Ruin and
Beauty: New and Selected Poems by Deena
Metzger (Red Hen Press, 2009). Reprinted
with permission of the author and
publisher.

229 Oscar Romero, translated by James R.
Brockman. From The Violence of Love,
translated by James R. Brockman. Reprinted
by permission of the Chicago Province of
the Society of Jesus. *

230 Barbara J. Pescan (UU). From "Memorial
Day Prayer" in Morning Watch (Skinner
House Books). *

231 Rabindranath Tagore. In The Complete
Poems of Rabindranath Tagore's Gitanjali:

Texts and Critical Evaluation by S. K. Paul (Sarup & Sons). *

232 Katherine Mosby. "Matins" in *The Book of Uncommon Prayer* by Katherine Mosby, whose works also include the award-winning novels *Private Altars*, *The Season of Lillian Dawes*, and *Twilight*, http://kmosby.com.

233 Langston Hughes. "Give Us Peace" from *The Collected Poems of Langston Hughes* by Langston Hughes, edited by Arnold Rampersad with David Roessel, Associate Editor, copyright © 1994 by the Estate of Langston Hughes. Used by permission of Alfred A. Knopf, an imprint of the Knopf Doubleday Publishing Group, a division of Penguin Random House LLC. All rights reserved.

234 Marcia Falk. "Blessing of Peace" in *The Book of Blessings: New Jewish Prayers for Daily Life, the Sabbath, and the New Moon Festival*, copyright © 1996 by Marcia Lee Falk. Used by permission of the author. *

235 Jean M. Rowe (UU). *

236 Orlanda Brugnola (UU). *

237 Upanishads. *

238 Patrick Murfin (UU). "Credo" in *We Build Temples in the Heart: Side by Side We Gather* (Skinner House Books). *

239 Rachel Naomi Remen. From *Kitchen Table Wisdom* (Riverhead Books). *

240 Gloria Anzaldúa. From *Borderlands/La Frontera* (Aunt Lute Books). *

241 Rainer Maria Rilke, translated by Stephen Mitchell. From "Letter 4" in *Letters to a Young Poet*, translated by Stephen Mitchell (Vintage). *

242 Joseph Campbell. From *The Hero with a Thousand Faces* (Pantheon Books). *

243 Kendyl Gibbons (UU). *

244 Chasidic prayer, translated by Chaim Stern. From *Day by Day*. Copyright © 1998 by the Central Conference of American Rabbis. *

245 Chaim Stern. From *Day by Day*. Copyright © 1998 by the Central Conference of American Rabbis. Reprinted by permission of Beacon Press, Boston.

246 Timothy Haley (UU). *

247 Orlanda Brugnola (UU). "As We Move" in *Voices from the Margins: An Anthology of Meditations*, edited by Jacqui James and Mark D. Morrison-Reed (Skinner House Books). *

248 Lisa Friedman (UU). *

249 Rita Dove. "Demeter's Prayer to Hades," from *Mother Love* by Rita Dove. Copyright © 1995 by Rita Dove. Used by permission of W.W. Norton & Company, Inc.

250 George G. Davis (UU). *

251 Nancy Shaffer (UU). "This Making of a Whole Self" in *Instructions in Joy* (Skinner House Books). *

252 Aryanto Nugroho (Unitarian). *

253 Boris Novak, translated by Mia Dintinjana. "Decisions II" by Boris Novak, translated by Mia Dintinjana, from *Fire in the Soul: 100 Poems for Human Rights*. Reprinted with permission from New Internationalist Publications, www.newint.org. *

Topical Index

Index of Authors and Translators

Index of First Lines and Titles

(When they differ, a piece's title, as well as its first line, is listed. Titles are in bold face.)

100